AIKIDO

AND

CHINESE MARTIAL ARTS

- Aikido and Weapons Training -

Written by

Tetsutaka Sugawara

Lujian Xing

Mark Jones

Translated into English from Chineseby Xuexiong Mei

(Dean of The Physical Education Department in Fujian Teachers' University)

Illustrations by Hironori Taniai

AIKIDO AND CHINESE MARTIAL ARTS - Aikido and Weapons Training

Written by Tetsutaka Sugawara, Lujian Xing, Mark Jones

ISBN: 0-87040-963-8

Translated into English from Chinese by Xuexiong Mei
Translated into English from Japanese by Eric Zmarzly (Ancient furnace and iron smelting)
proofreading by Patrick Nicols

Edited by Tetsutaka Sugawara, Mark Jones

Illustrations by Hironori Taniai

Copyright

©1998 by Tetsutaka Sugawara, Lujian Xing, Mark Jones

Published by

SUGAWARA MARTIAL ARTS INSTITUTE, INC.

20-13, Tadao 3 Chome, Machida-Shi, Tokyo 194-0035 Japan

Phone: (0427)94-0972 / FAX: (0427) 94-0899

E-mail: tsugawar@ga2.so-net.ne.jp

First printing: May 1998

Printed in Japan

DISTRIBUTORS

United States: Kodansha America, Inc. through Oxford University Press, 198 Madison Avenue, New York, NY 10016.

Canada: Fitzhenry & Whiteside Ltd., 195 Allstate Parkway, Markham, Ontario L3R 4T8.

United Kingdom and Europe: Premier Book Marketing Ltd., 1 Gower Street, London WC1E 6HA.

Australia and New Zealand: Bookwise International, 54 Crittenden Road, Findon, South Australia 5023.

The Far East and Japan: Japan Publications Trading Co., Ltd., 1-2-1, Sarugaku-cho, Chiyoda-ku, Tokyo 101-0064, Japan.

AIKIDO
AND
CHINESE MARTIAL ARTS
- Aikido and Weapons Training -

Introduction

In this volume, we take up the theme, "how to use weapons in Aikido and Chinese martial arts".
Through weapons training, you will be able to understand about the following martial arts elements:

(1) The difference between body techniques and weapons training

(2) The difference between the Japanese curved sword, and the Chinese straight sword

(3) How to take a proper distance

(4) How to watch your partner's eyes

(5) How to grab your partner's mind

(6) How to move with good timing

(7) Proper traditional foot work

(8) Circular movements with the weapon

(9) A block should include an attack, an attack should include a block

(10) Long weapon's, and short weapon's weak points

(11) The weak points of armor

(12) How ancient people produced good steel about two thousand years ago with little technology.

In our training, we must vow to take responsibility not to use weapons for disreputable reasons. Our purpose of Japanese/Chinese weapons training should be for lifelong study and good health. Also, I challenge the readers to try and smelt their own iron and attempt to produce swords.

Tetsutaka Sugawara

March 15th, 1998

Sword History in Japan

Bronze sword.
From Ukikunden Site, Karatsu-shi, Saga.
Yayoi Period, 2nd-1st century B.C.
Karatsu-shi Uki-ku, Township, Saga

Bronze sword with handle.
From Yoshinogari Site, Mitagawa-cho, Kanzaki,
Kanzaki-gun, Saga.
Yayoi Period, 1st century B.C.
Agency for Cultural Affairs.

Iron sword.
From Futatsukayama Site, Kamimine-mura,
Miyagi-gun and Higashiseburi-mura, Kanzaki-gun,
Saga.
Yayoi Period, 1st-2nd century.
Saga Prefectural Museum.

Undulating sword.
From Kuwa No. 57 Tumulus, Oyama-shi, Tochigi.
Kofun Period, 5th century.
Oyama-shi Edication Commision, Chiba.

Sword with ring pommel with double dragon
ornament and gilt bronze fittings.
From Matsumen Tumulus, Kisarazu-shi, Chiba.
Kofun Period, 6th century.
Tokyo National Museum.

Sword with round pommel and silver inlay
decoration.
From Hirai-chiku No. 1 Tumulus, Fujioka-shi,
Gunma.
Kofun Period, 6th century.
Fujioka-shi Education Commission, Gunma.

Sword with bulbous pommel and gilt bronze
fittings.
From Watanuki Kannon'yama Tumulus, Taksaki-
shi, Gunma.
Kofun Period, 6th century.
Agency for Cultural Affairs.

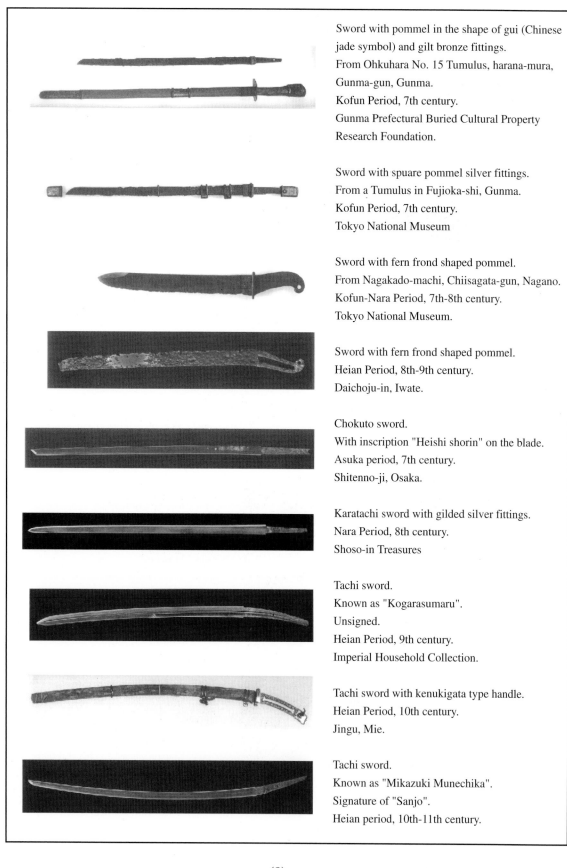

Sword with pommel in the shape of gui (Chinese jade symbol) and gilt bronze fittings.
From Ohkuhara No. 15 Tumulus, harana-mura, Gunma-gun, Gunma.
Kofun Period, 7th century.
Gunma Prefectural Buried Cultural Property Research Foundation.

Sword with spuare pommel silver fittings.
From a Tumulus in Fujioka-shi, Gunma.
Kofun Period, 7th century.
Tokyo National Museum

Sword with fern frond shaped pommel.
From Nagakado-machi, Chiisagata-gun, Nagano.
Kofun-Nara Period, 7th-8th century.
Tokyo National Museum.

Sword with fern frond shaped pommel.
Heian Period, 8th-9th century.
Daichoju-in, Iwate.

Chokuto sword.
With inscription "Heishi shorin" on the blade.
Asuka period, 7th century.
Shitenno-ji, Osaka.

Karatachi sword with gilded silver fittings.
Nara Period, 8th century.
Shoso-in Treasures

Tachi sword.
Known as "Kogarasumaru".
Unsigned.
Heian Period, 9th century.
Imperial Household Collection.

Tachi sword with kenukigata type handle.
Heian Period, 10th century.
Jingu, Mie.

Tachi sword.
Known as "Mikazuki Munechika".
Signature of "Sanjo".
Heian period, 10th-11th century.

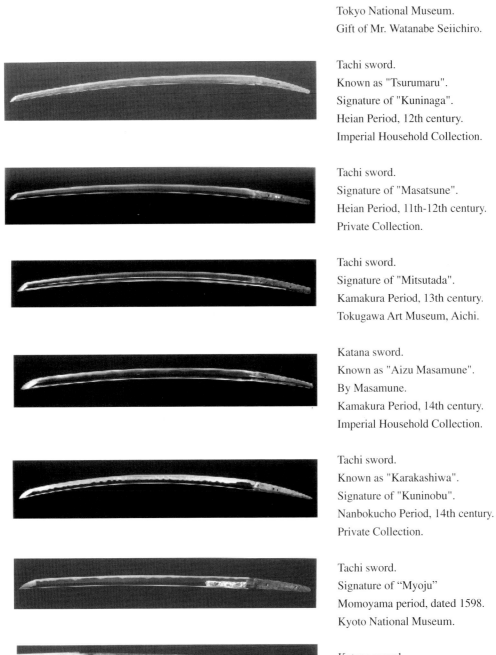

Tokyo National Museum.
Gift of Mr. Watanabe Seiichiro.

Tachi sword.
Known as "Tsurumaru".
Signature of "Kuninaga".
Heian Period, 12th century.
Imperial Household Collection.

Tachi sword.
Signature of "Masatsune".
Heian Period, 11th-12th century.
Private Collection.

Tachi sword.
Signature of "Mitsutada".
Kamakura Period, 13th century.
Tokugawa Art Museum, Aichi.

Katana sword.
Known as "Aizu Masamune".
By Masamune.
Kamakura Period, 14th century.
Imperial Household Collection.

Tachi sword.
Known as "Karakashiwa".
Signature of "Kuninobu".
Nanbokucho Period, 14th century.
Private Collection.

Tachi sword.
Signature of "Myoju"
Momoyama period, dated 1598.
Kyoto National Museum.

Katana sword.
Signature "Masahide".
Edo Period, 18th century.
The Japanese Sword Museum, Tokyo.

(From "Nihon no Katana", Tokyo National Museum, 1998)

The process of making Japanese sword by Taira Sugawara, sword-smith

Sand iron

Iron stone

Tamahagane

See Appendix

- Contents -

Part One: Aikido Weapons Training

Chapter 1. Basic Knowledge of Weapons

1. How to grip the sword

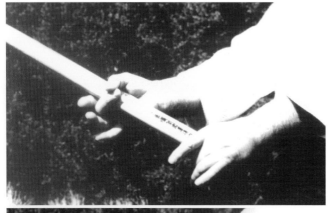

First touch your thumb and middle finger and then grip with all your fingers.

The space between both hands is the width of one fist. Therefore, your grip is a total of three fists width. It is very important not to change this width when you are practising.

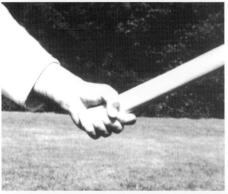

Hold your left hand at the end of the sword handle, as shown in photo.

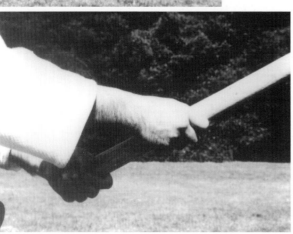

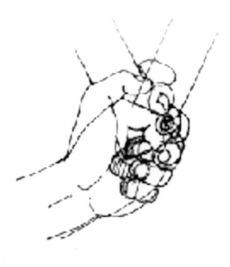

Naturally extend the right arm a little.

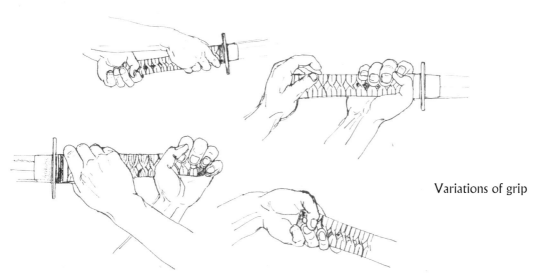

Variations of grip

Poor grip

These are examples of bad grips. The upper photo shows that you can't turn your wrists smoothly, like in the above movements.

The lower photo shows that when your sword is struck, you easily loose your grip.

2. Makiuchi strike

From the Seigan stance, raise your bokken with both hands, with the left hand going up faster than your right hand. Then focus your mind at the tip of the sword and aim for your partner's forehead for a strike.

Fig. 1

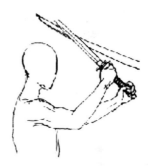

Fig. 2

Fig. 4

Fig. 5

Kenshin Uesugi's Haramaki

(Muromachi Era, owner:Uesugi Shrine)

(From the "Zukai Nihon Kacchu Jiten" p. 76, Yusan-kaku, 1976)

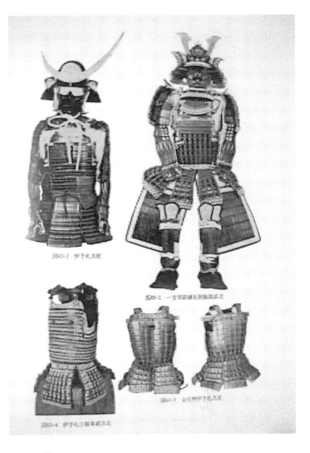

Gusoku

(Azuchi-Momoyama Era)

(From the "Zukai Nihon Kacchu Jiten", Yusan-kaku, 1976)

When you wear the helmet protector, you should strike with *makiuchi* style, because you can't raise both arms to the top of your head.

See above protector.

3. How to grip the Jo

3.1. An example of the correct grip

Yang grip

Yin grip

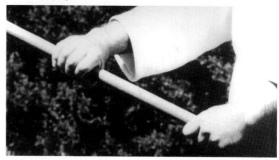

Upper photo is yang, which is the same as the sword grip.

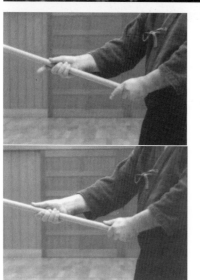

An example of a bad grip.

3.2. How to change your grip yin and yang

The next page shows how to change your grip from yin to yang quickly, and smoothly (Left side illustrations on next page).

Rub both palms along the jo, and change your grip from the left to the right side. Do not separate your grip thumb from the jo when changing (Right side illustrations on next page).

Change the grip

Change the direction

3.3. How to Strike and block

Strike from the shoulders, tightening your back muscles. Then, strike by twisting your hip, arm extended, concentrating your mind on the tip of the jo. Aim at your partner's weak point.

Extend you body

3.3.1. Strike from the stance

When you strike from any kamae (stance), you should concentrate your mind between the tip of your weapon, and the weak point of your partner's body, and then attack quickly. Your mind, foot, and hand must move as one single movement.

The next illustration show the direction of attacks.

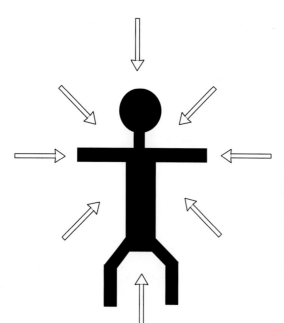

3.3.2. The three elements

Very important is the combination of the three elements: mind concentration, breathing, and the muscles. This is said in Japanese as *shin* (mind), *gi* (techniques), and *tai* (body) *no icchi* (fit).

If you grip loosely, or raise it without purpose, you can't realize the combination of these three elements.

3.3.3. Poor striking

When you strike from the shoulder stance, do not change your jo from the shoulder level. This photo shows the jo separated from the shoulders by loosening the back muscles. This type of striking becomes very slow.

3.3.4. Tsuke

After attacking with the jo, you should put your jo on your partner's centerline. Usually, tsuke is a middle level stance (seigan).

3.3.5. Block and thrust

Put the tip of the sword on the centerline when blocking. Then, you can thrust, if you slide the tip of your sword to your partner's lower level.

3.3.6. Tatezue-no-Kamae

There are two styles, one is with your Jo vertical in front of your left toe, and vertical, but a little to the right side in front of your left toe. If you wait for your partner's attack, and show your weak point (wrist), you give your easy strike to your wrist. Therefore, from this stance, you should train repeatedly to move quickly to the right and left, or front and back.

From this stance, you should train for a counter attack when your partner attacks. You should grip the upper or lower part of the jo with your right hand.

3.3.7. Straight thrust

When you take up a jo, concentrate your mind on the tip. Then, thrust straight to your partner's weak point. Make sure that your jo tip travels in a straight line to the target, and does not wander about.

Also, you should use good body extended twisting your hip, arms extended, and slide the jo through your lead hand. Rock your body forward by bending your front knee. Aim the tip of your jo at the nearest target. Remember to keep good posture. Return the jo to the starting position faster than you thrust it.

3.3.8. Target

Some of the main targets for thrusting are shown with the following illustration.

In the beginning, you should aim at only one position with the straight thrust. Concentrate your mind on the tip of the jo.

Later, is double thrust training. For instance, if you aimed at the upper level with a forward thrust, then thrust at the middle level the second time.

The next method is to thrust to the left and right sides.

The last method is feint thrusting, such as if you

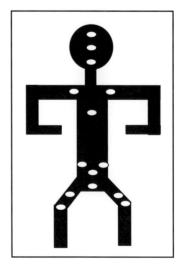

aimed at the lower level, then thrust first at the upper level and then quickly changed to the lower level.

4. How to use the sword

In Japanese martial arts, there are some sword cutting methods as follows;

1. Nuki-uchi: From the taiken-no-kamae, draw the sword and attack vertically from the head level.

2. Nuki-tsuke: From the taiken-no-kamae, draw the sword and attack horizontally.

3. Kesa-giri: A downward diagonal cut from the neck to the other side of the abdomen. Use the sword tip about 10 cm.

4. Shomen-uchi: Front head strike, or straight thrust with the tip of the sword to the forehead.

5. Yokomen-uchi: Side head strike, or pushing strike, using the sword tip about 10 cm or so.

6. Hara-zuki: Thrust through the abdomen. Lay down the sword edge horizontally to the left (right foot steps in) or right (left foot steps in).

7. Nuki-do: Push and slice the partner's abdomen. You should have both wrists crossed and put power in the sword tip. Concentrate your power to the whole blade and pull across the abdomen.

8. Shinzo-tsuki: Pointing thrust to the heart with the tip of the sword., or thrust through. Use the sword edge perpendicularly.

9. Kote-uchi: Wrist strike. Attack the partner's inside wrist with the tip of the sword about 20 cm or so.

10. Kubi-uchi: Neck cutting. Use the sword horizontally with a pushing slice. Use most of the sword edge.

11. Men-sashi (or Sashi-men): Thrusting at the face. The main weak point are on the centerline of the face.

12. Uchi-mata-giri: Inside of both legs. Cut the inside of the leg with the all of the edge.

Usually, when you cut, you should aim at two targets using the tip of the sword for the strike, and use all of the blade to slice in one beat (for instance,

the wrist and the abdomen). Or you should execute cutting to the neck and abdomen in one continuous, circular cut.

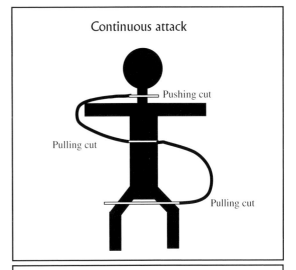

Continuous attack

Pushing cut

Pulling cut

Pulling cut

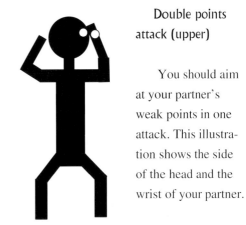

Double points attack (upper)

You should aim at your partner's weak points in one attack. This illustration shows the side of the head and the wrist of your partner.

Double points attack (lower)

You should aim at your partner's weak points in one attack. This illustration shows the wrist and the lower side of the abdomen of your partner.

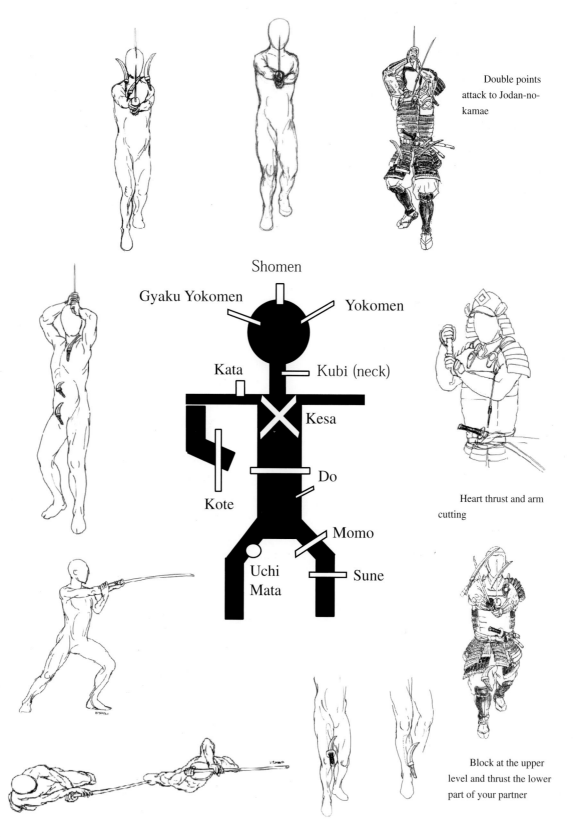

Double points attack to Jodan-no-kamae

Shomen

Gyaku Yokomen

Yokomen

Kata

Kubi (neck)

Kesa

Do

Kote

Momo

Uchi Mata

Sune

Heart thrust and arm cutting

Block at the upper level and thrust the lower part of your partner

5. The principles of Martial Arts

3.1. Mokujin 木人 (wood-man)

This is a Chinese principle. If you were attacked on your left side, counter attack with the right side at the same time. If you were attacked at the upper part of your body, counter attack with the lower part of

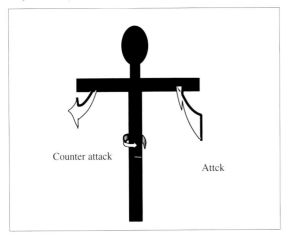

Counter attack

Attck

your body.

3.2. Shin 伸 (*Shen* in Chinese)

This is a Chinese principle. Shin means an "extension of the body". If you could extend your body by bending your knee, extending your shoulder and arms, you can make the distance closer and attack more efficiently against your enemy (See Vol. 1 of Aikido and Chinese Martial Arts).

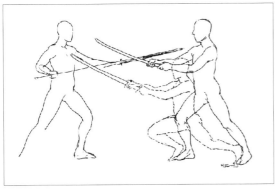

3.3. Sha 卸 (*Xie* in Chinese)

This is a Chinese principle. Xie means "quick downward shift of the body". When you attack, bend your knee quickly to extend your body. But usually, your body rises up first before going down. You should discard this waste movement.

3.4. Ippo 一歩, or one step

The traditional step is the same as natural walking step. For instance, when you step with the right foot forward in one strike, avoid moving your left foot backward (usually step back a little bit). Discard this waste movement. If you are upset, usually your waste movements are apparent.

If you moved both feet at the same time, this is the same as one step. You can change your hanmi stance with this step to the other hanmi stance. But, your hand work must fit with one step.

3.5. Issoku Itto 一足一刀, Fit one step to one strike

When making a makiuchi strike, if you raise your hands and strike down in one beat, this hand work fits in one step. But if you raise your hand in one beat and strike with second beat, your foot work stops and has to wait for your strike. That is an inefficient strike.

3.6. Aiki 合気 or Ki-ken-tai-no-icchi 気剣体の一致, Fit ki (mind), ken (sword) and Tai (body)

If your ki (mind, or concentration to the sword tip), step, and hand work, are coordinated with your breathing, your power increases. That is why your ki controls the weapon, breathing, stepping, and your hands.

6. Circular attack and block

6.1. Spiral block

This is a blocking movement against your partner's jo to the left and right side with a diagonal step in.

6.2. Spiral block and attack

After block your partner's jo to the left, thrust quickly his/her weak point.

6.3. Circular jo training with yang grip

Fig. 1, 2, 3, 4

Fig. 5, 6, 7

6.4. Partner practice

Jo blocks the swordsman's attack with a spiral motion, and then thrusts continuously to the lower part of the partner's body.

Jo can't guard his neck if his jo is separated from the sword. In a spiral motion, never let the weapons lose contact with each other.

6.5. Circular block with sword

7. Kamae and the level of the tip of weapons

7.1. Various types of Seigan-no-kamae (middle level stance)

Kumijo #1-4
Omote-no-seigan (The nose level)

7.2. Gedan or Gyaku Gedan-no-kamae (The knee level)

a. Gedan-no-kamae

From seigan-no-kamae, lower the tip of the weapon to the knee level.

b. Gyaku Gedan-no-kamae

In left hanmi, lower the tip of the weapon to the knee level.

Kumijo # 5-8
Ura-no-seigan (The solar plexus level)

Jo-ai # 1-5
Oku-no-Seigan (The chest level)
This is the half way between Omote and Ura-no-seigan. (There is no photograph)

Kumijo #5-8
Ura-no-seigan (The solar plexus level)

7.3. In (Yin)-no-kamae (The ear level)

lose this strong meaning, because from the Gedan stance, thrusting may be faster than from Jodan.

Point your sword straight up with the blade facing your partner. The position of your right wrist should be level to your right ear. Stand with your sword straight, and position it to the inside of your body like a shadow, keep your upper body straight. This stance is called "In stance". It means a shadow, which is the same as Yin in Chinese. By using this "In stance", you can show your strong mind to the opponent, and you can attack quickly.

7.4. Jodan-no-kamae (The head level)

"Jodan" is the upper (head) level. In this stance,

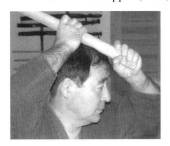

you can show your strong mind to your opponent, but if the opponent takes Gedan (lower) stance, Jodan may

7.5. Sha-no-kamae

From the seigan-no-kamae, your right foot steps back with the tip of the weapon to the rear. The abdomen is facing to the right, but your head is facing to the front.

"Sha" means "throw away". If you throw your life away in your mind, you become strong. This stance exposes all of your body to your opponent who can attack easily, but you can read his intent to achieve a winning strike.

8. Block

8.1. Chudan level block with sword

When attacked at your chest or wrist, make a triangle shape with the sword and the arm. Then, block the strike with your body, put the sword tip on the centerline between you and your partner's center.

Keep your sword tip in line with your partner's nose.

8.2. Chudan level block with jo

Block your jo at a right-angle to your partner's

weapon, because you must avoid having your partner's weapon slip to your wrist.

If your distance is close to your partner, you

8.3. Upper level block

If you were attacked yokomen (side of the head), block the weapon by the same movement of 8.1, but the level higher.

8.5. Block the neck

Block your neck by entering with your right foot to the right front with your arms extend to the front at shoulder level. Be sure to watch for a continued attack by your partner to your abdomen or legs, after your block.

8.4. Sword strike with jo

Strike as if to break the attacker's sword. Return the jo to your partner's nose level after the strike.

Chapter 2: Hard style Kumijo (Sword vs Jo)

Kumijo #1

Fig. 1

Fig. 2

Fig. 3

Fig. 4

Standing Bow
(Figs. 1-9)

The standing bow begins with both partners facing each other approximately twelve feet apart. In these practices the sword side will be referred to as the uketachi and the jo side as the uchikomi.

The uketachi holds the sword with the left hand at the height of the belt with the handle facing forward and the cutting edge up (Fig. 1).

The uchikomi holds the jo with the left hand positioned in the center of the jo and tucks it under the left armpit (Fig.1).

24

Fig. 5

Fig. 6

Fig. 7

Fig. 8

Fig. 9

Both partners bow towards each other then take two steps forward, first with the left foot, then with the right foot (Figs. 2-7). At the same time as the first step, uketachi pulls the sword forward with the left hand and places the back of the right hand on the side of the sword handle with the cutting edge facing away from the body (Figs. 2-4). As the uketachi steps with the right foot, the right hand draws the sword up as the left hand slides down the sword to the belt. The sword continues in a circular path, finishing in front of the body with the left hand at the end of the handle, little finger half on half off (Figs. 5-8).

At the same time the uketachi is stepping and drawing the sword, uchikomi steps with the left foot and draws the jo out with the left hand (Figs. 2, 3). The right hand reaches under the jo and behind the left hand, gripping about three hand widths from the end of the jo (Figs. 3, 4). As the uchikomi steps with the right foot, the left hand slides over the right hand gripping end of the jo with no overlap of the little finger (Figs. 5-8).

Fig. 10

Fig. 11

Fig. 12

Fig. 13

The uketachi decides the distance, then the uchikomi adjusts forward or backward to achieve the correct distance (ma-ai) (Fig. 10, 11).

The uketachi moves first, stepping backwards with the right foot and assuming sha-no-kamae. The uchikomi moves immediatly after the uketachi moves, stepping up with his left foot, toe to toe, then back with his right foot, neither gaining nor losing distance.The jo is stood upright, then slides through the left hand to the ground just inside the left foot (Figs. 14-17). The left wrist is bent inward to offer the wrist as a target for the uketachi.

Fig. 14

Fig. 15

Fig. 16

Fig. 17

Without taking a step, the uketachi raises up to hidari jodan no kamae (Figs. 18-21).

Fig. 18

Fig. 19

Fig. 20

Fig. 21

The uketachi then steps up with the right foot, toe to toe, while at the same time cutting down with the sword (Figs. 22-25).

Fig. 22

Fig. 23

Fig. 24

Fig. 25

The uketachi then proceeds to cut the uchikomi's wrist with a maki uchi (Figs. 26-30).

Fig. 26

Fig. 27

Fig. 28

Fig. 29

Fig. 30

Fig. 31

Fig. 32

Fig. 33

The uchikomi steps with the right foot to the right while rotating the left hand and finishing with the jo on top of the sword (Figs. 30-32).

Fig. 34

Fig. 35

Fig. 36

Fig. 37

The uchikomi then steps with the left foot straight towards the uketachi, thrusting at the uketachi's solar plexus (Figs. 33, 34). The jo slides smoothly through the left hand with power being supplied by the right hand, angling upwards from low to high.

The uketachi steps back with the right foot while blocking to the left (Figs. 34,35). A triangle is created with the tip of the sword on the centerline, the body, and the left hand (?).

The uketachi steps forward with the right foot, sliding the sword down the jo, keeping the tip on the centerline and then cutting the waist (Figs 35-37).

The uchikomi slides back, stepping first with the right foot, then with the left foot; remaining in left hanmi. At the same time, the tip of the jo drops down in a clockwise motion, with the back of the right hand touching the top of the forehead. The sword is blocked on the left side of the uchikomi (Figs. 35-37).

Fig. 38

The uchikomi then steps again to the right, putting most of the weight on the right foot. At the same time, the jo circles around in a clockwise motion, striking down on top the sword (Figs. 38-40).

Fig. 39

With the left foot, the uchikomi steps forward, thrusting at the face (Figs. 41, 42).

Fig. 40

Fig. 41

33

Fig. 42

Fig. 43

Fig. 44

Fig. 45

The uketachi once more steps back with the right foot and blocks towards the left, slightly higher than before (Figs. 42-44).

Once again the uketachi enters with the right foot, cutting the left side of the uchikomi at waist level (Figs. 45-49).

The uchikomi repeats the earlier block by sliding backwards while circling the jo clockwise from underneath and touching the back of the right hand to the forehead (Figs. 46-49).

Fig. 46

Fig. 47

Fig. 48

Fig. 49

The uketachi slides back with the left foot, followed by the right foot, and drops the sword to gedan with the tip of the sword on the centerline (Figs. 49, 50).

Fig. 50

The uchikomi raises the jo over the head, bringing the hands together at the center of the jo. The right hand rotates the jo, while the left hand slides over the right hand, down to the end of the jo. At the same time, the right foot steps forward and the uchikomi strikes with the jo at the left side of the uketachi's head, yoko-menuchi (Figs. 50-53).

Fig. 51

Fig. 52

The uketachi holds position while raising the sword up, keeping the tip on the centerline and the hands extending to the left (Figs. 51-53).

Fig. 53

When the jo is blocked, the uchikomi steps back and to the right while withdrawing the jo. The uchikomi pivots forward, stepping with the left foot, pulling with the right hand while extending with the left hand, and striking the uketachi at the knee (Figs. 54-59).

Fig. 54

Fig. 55

The uketachi steps back with the right foot, evading the knee strike while raising the sword and cutting in a counter-clockwise motion, striking downward at the jo (Fig. 57-60).

Fig. 56

Fig. 57

37

Fig. 58

Fig. 59

Fig. 60

After the uchikomi is blocked, rotate the jo by holding it with the left hand and sliding the right hand over the left to the other end of the jo, finishing in the thrusting posture, tsuki-no-kamae (Figs. 61-63).

Fig. 61

As the uchikomi recovers, the uketachi steps back with the left foot and strikes with maki-uchi, finishing with the basic sword posture, ken-no-kamae (Figs. 61-64).

Fig. 62

Both sides remain focused and motionless for 3 to 4 seconds. This is the unbroken concentration at the end of a technique, called zanshin (Fig. 65).

Fig. 63

Fig. 64

Fig. 65

Kumijo #2

Fig. 1

Fig. 2

Fig. 3

Fig. 4

Before this movements, inset the Kumijo #1 Fig. 10 -25.

The second partner pactice starts out the same as the first practice with the exception that the uchikomi has the jo in front of the foot instead of inside.

Uketachi steps with the right foot and cuts toward the head with makiuchi. It is not necessary to reach the head of the uchikomi (Figs. 2-4).

The uchikomi steps back with the right foot, grasping the jo from over the top with the right hand. The jo comes up in a clockwise motion, striking the sword on its side (Figs. 4-7).

Fig. 5

Fig. 6

Fig. 7

Uketachi drops to the lower postion (gedan), while keeping the tip of the sword on the centerline (Fig. 8).

Fig. 8

With the sword in the lower position the uchikomi now has an opening in the upper position. Bringing the jo up over the head with the hands together, the left hand slides down the jo until it reaches the end. The uchikomi steps forward and strikes the uketachi in the side of the head (yoko-menuchi) (Figs. 8, 9). Uketachi raises the sword up to receive the jo, keeping the tip on the centerline and extending to the left (Figs. 10, 11).

Fig. 9

Fig.10

Fig.11

Fig.12

After the jo is blocked, the uchikomi withdrawns the jo, at the same time stepping back and to the left, left foot then right foot (Figs.11,12).

At the same time the uchikomi steps sideways, uketachi drops the sword to gedan, pivoting slightly to the right while keeping the tip of the sword on uchikomi's centerline (Fig. 12).

Fig.13

Uchikomi steps forward with the left foot, striking the uketachi in the side of the right knee (gedan gaeshi) (Figs. 13-16).

Fig.14

The uketachi steps back with the right foot, cutting with a counter clockwise motion, blocking the jo (Figs. 14-16).

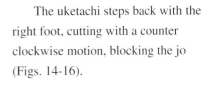

Fig.15

Fig.16

43

Fig. 17

Fig. 18

Fig. 19

Fig. 20

The uketachi steps forward with the right foot, cutting the left wrist of the uchikomi (Figs. 17-19).

Uchikomi evades by stepping to the right with the right foot, sliding the right hand down the jo while rotating the left hand, stiking the back of the sword (Figs. 18,19).

The uchikomi then steps forward with the left foot, thrusting at the solar plexus of the uketachi (Figs. 20-23).

Uketachi steps back with the right foot and blocks to the left, keeping the tip of the sword on the centerline and extending the hands to the left (Figs 21-23).

Fig. 21

Fig. 22

Fig. 23

Fig. 24

Fig. 25

The uketachi steps forward with the right foot, sliding the sword down the jo, keeping the tip on the centerline and cutting the waist (Figs 24-27).

Fig. 26

Fig. 27

The uchikomi slides back, stepping first with the right foot, then with the left foot and remaining in left hanmi. At the same time, the tip of the jo drops down in a clockwise motion with the back of the right hand touching the top of the forehead. The sword is blocked on the left side of the uchikomi (Figs. 25-28).

Fig. 28

Uketachi slides
backwards, stepping first
with the left foot, then the
right, dropping the sword
into gedan (Figs.28-30).

Fig. 29

Fig. 30

The uchikomi raises the
jo over the head, bringing
the hands together at the
center of the jo. The right
hand rotates the jo, while the
left hand slides over the right
down to the end of the jo. At
the same time, the uchikomi
steps forward with the right
foot and strikes with the jo at
the left side of the uketachi's
head, yoko-menuchi (Figs.
30-33).

Fig. 31

Fig. 32

Fig. 33

As the uchikomi attacks with yokomen uchi, uketachi enters diagonally with the right foot, sword extended in front, with the tip towards the right. After meeting the jo with the cutting edge, the uketachi steps with the left foot, pivoting the right foot behind while cutting the waist of the uchikomi (Figs. 33-40).

Fig. 34

Fig. 35

When the uketachi enters to cut the waist, the uchikomi steps with the left foot and pivots the right foot around in the same manner as the uketachi (Figs. 35-40). At the same time, uchikomi holds the jo with the right hand, slides the left hand over the right while rotating the jo counter clockwise, bringing the right hand to the top of the forehead and blocking the sword cut to the waist (Figs. 36-40).

Fig. 36

Fig. 37

Fig. 38

Fig. 39

Fig. 40

Change the both grips swiftly
and turn your body to the right.

49

The uchikomi then drops the right hand from the forehead to a position just in front of the right shoulder with the palm of the right hand facing forward (Figs.41-43).

Fig. 41

The uketachi drops the sword from waist level to the lower position with the left foot forward (gyaku gedan) (Figs. 41-43).

Fig. 42

Fig. 43

Uketachi steps forward with the right foot and attacks uchikomi's head with maki-uchi (Figs. 44-47).

Fig. 44

Uchikomi steps back with the right foot only while snapping the end of the jo up in a clockwise motion, striking the sword on the side (Figs. 46-48).

Fig. 45

Fig. 46

Fig. 47

Fig. 48

Uketachi slides backwards, first with the left foot, followed by the right and finishing with a maki-uchi (Figs. 49-52).

Fig. 49

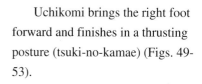

Uchikomi brings the right foot forward and finishes in a thrusting posture (tsuki-no-kamae) (Figs. 49-53).

Fig. 50

Fig. 51

Fig. 52

Fig. 53

Kumijo #3

Fig. 1

Fig. 2

Fig. 3

Fig. 4

Uketachi will initiate the same as the first and second kumijo (Figs. 1-5). At the same time as theuketachi moves into sha-no-kamae, uchikomi does the same (Figs. 1-4).

Fig. 5

As the uketachi cuts towards the head, the uchikomi steps forward and to the left with the right foot, bringing the left hand to the top of the forehead and cutting underneath the sword with the jo (Figs. 5, 6).

The uketachi then slides back and drops the sword to gedan with the tip on the centerline (Figs. 7, 8).

Fig. 6

After uketachi drops the sword to gedan, uchikomi steps forward with the left foot, rotating the jo from the right side, up and over the head, attacking the uketachi with a strike to the top of the head (shomen-uchi) (Figs. 7-10).

Fig. 7

Fig. 8

Fig. 9

Fig. 10

The uketachi steps back with the right foot while blocking the jo to the left, with the tip of the sword slightly to the left of center (Figs. 8-10). The uketachi then steps forward with the left foot, cutting the left leg of the uchikomi (Figs. 11-14).

Fig. 11

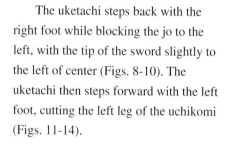

Fig. 12

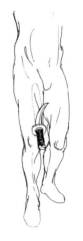

When the uketachi
attacks the leg, the
uchikomi steps back and to
the right, withdrawing the
jo and evading the strike
(Figs. 12-14).

Fig. 13

Fig. 14

Fig. 15

Fig. 16

The uchikomi steps
forward with the right foot
and attacks the left leg of
the uketachi with gedan
gaeshi (Figs. 15-18).

The uketachi evades by
stepping backwards with
the left foot.while cutting in
a clockwise circle to meet
the jo in gedan (Figs. 16-
18).

Fig. 17

Fig. 18

The uketachi steps forward with the right foot and cuts the top of the uchikomi's right wrist with a small circular cut (Figs. 19-21).

Fig. 19

The uchikomi evades by stepping back and to the left, while the jo pivots in a clockwise motion, striking down on the back of the sword (Figs. 19-21).

Fig. 20

Fig. 21

Fig. 22

Fig. 23

Fig. 24

The uchikomi thrusts towards the solar plexus of uketachi while stepping forward with the right foot (Figs. 22-24).

The uketachi extends the sword to the right, keeping the tip of the sword on the centerline without moving the feet. A triangle is created between the tip of the sword, the left hand, and the uketachi's centerline (Figs. 22-24).

Fig. 25

The uketachi slides the sword down the jo and steps in with the left foot, executing a strike to uchikomi's right side (Figs. 25-28).

Fig. 26

Fig. 27

The uchikomi slides back, stepping first with the left foot, then with the right. The jo circles counter clockwise from underneath, with the left hand touching the top of the forehead, blocking the sword (Figs. 26-28).

Fig. 28

Fig. 29

Fig. 30

Fig. 31

Fig. 32

Uchikomi steps to the left and back with the left foot, while bringing the jo around the sword and striking down on the side of the sword (Figs. 29-31).

Uchikomi steps forward with the right foot and thrusts at the face of uketachi (Figs. 32-34).

Uketachi pivots on the left foot, bringing the sword up and blocking the jo with the back of the sword, finishing with the left foot forward and the sword over the head, hidari jodan-no-kamae (Figs. 31-35).

Fig. 33

Fig. 34

After the jo is blocked, uchikomi slides back and drops the tip of the jo to the gedan with the tip on the uketachi's centerline, (Figs. 35-37).

Fig. 35

Fig. 36

Fig. 37

Fig. 38

Fig. 39

Fig. 40

Uketachi steps forward with the right foot, striking straight down on uchikomi's head (Figs. 38-41)

As the sword comes down, uchikomi steps to the left with the left foot then the right, with the right foot finishing behind the left. At the same time the right hand slides about two thirds of the way down the jo and the left hand one third of the way down (Figs. 40, 41).

Fig. 41

The left hand comes up and over, striking down with the jo on the back of the sword. The left hand continues the jo in a circular path with the right hand holding on. The left hand slides down the jo over the right hand to the end of the jo. The right hand will switch from thumb down to thumb up, finishing with the jo in a vertical position, hasso-no-kamae (Figs. 41-45).

Fig. 42

Fig. 43

After the sword is blocked, uketachi slides back, dropping the sword to gedan with the tip on uchikomi's centerline (Figs. 43-45).

Fig. 44

Fig. 45

Fig. 46

Fig. 47

Uchikomi steps forward with the right foot and strikes uketachi on the left side of the head, yokomen-uchi (Figs. 47-50).

Fig. 48

Uketachi raises the sword up with the tip on the centerline and the hands extending to the left, receiving the strike (Figs. 48, 49).

Fig. 49

Fig. 50

After the jo is blocked, uchikomi makes a small clockwise motion with the tip of the jo coming to the height of uketachi's solar plexus (Figs. 51, 52).

Fig. 51

When the jo moves away from the sword, uketachi will slide back and finish with a maki-uchi (Figs. 51-53).

Fig. 52

Fig. 53

The uchikomi brings the tip of the jo up to the level of the sword (Figs. 54, 55).

Fig. 54

Fig. 55

Kumijo #4

Fig. 1

Uketachi and uchikomi start from a mutual sword stance with the right foot forward (Fig. 1).

Fig. 1

Fig. 3

Uketachi initiates by walking forward, first with the left foot then the right. At the same time uchikomi walks backwards two steps, keeping the same distance (ma-ai) (Figs. 2-8).

Fig. 4

Fig. 5

Fig. 6

Fig. 7

Fig. 8

Fig. 9

Fig. 10

Fig. 11

Fig. 12

After both partners have taken their two steps, uchikomi adjusts the distance as it might have changed during the walk (Figs. 9, 10).

Uketachi then steps back with the right foot into the posture of in-no-kamae where the sword is held in a vertical position, right hand at eye level and cutting edge pointing towards uchikomi's centerline (Figs.11-16).

Fig. 13

Fig. 14

Fig. 15

Fig. 16

At the same time as uketachi takes in-no-kamae, uchikomi steps up with the left foot, toe to toe, then back with the right foot, making sure distance has not been changed. Uchikomi changes from a sword posture into a thrusting posture by sliding the left hand over the right and the right hand down to the end of the jo (Figs.12-17).

Fig. 17

Fig. 18

Fig. 19

Fig. 20

The uchikomi steps forward with the right foot while bringing the right hand to the top of the forehead (Figs. 20-23). Uchikomi then steps with the left foot and thrust towards the left shoulder of uketachi (Figs. 24-26).

Fig. 21

Fig. 22

Fig. 23

Fig. 24

As the uchikomi moves forward, the uketachi moves backwards, matching uchikomi step for step. When uchikomi thrusts at the shoulder, uketachi cuts to the left, deflecting the jo and taking the centerline (Figs. 21-27).

Fig. 25

Fig. 26

Fig. 27

Uketachi raises the sword over the head to hidari jodan-no-kamae (Figs. 28, 29).

Fig. 28

With the sword in the upper position, the uchikomi steps forward with the right foot, going down on to the left knee, and striking the outside of uketachi's left knee (Figs. 29-32).

Fig. 29

Fig. 30

Fig. 31

Uketachi steps back with the left foot while cutting down on the inside (left side) of the jo (Figs. 31-33).

Fig. 32

Fig. 33

Fig. 34

Fig. 35

Fig. 36

After the uketachi blocks the jo, the sword is turned so the cutting edge is facing down and the tip is on the centerline (Figs. 33, 34).

The uchikomi withdraws the jo, then steps up with the left foot, drawing the jo up through the left hand, and thrusting towards the face (Figs. 34-37).

The uketachi blocks towards the right, keeping the tip on the centerline and extending the hands to the right (Figs. 36, 37).

Fig. 37

Fig. 38

Fig. 39

Fig. 40

Uchikomi then steps to the right with the right foot only, while rotating the jo with the left hand, sliding the right hand from one end of the jo to the other, and strikes the sword (Figs 38-40).

The uchikomi steps forward with the left foot and thrusts once more at the face (Figs. 41, 42).

Uketachi allows the force of the jo on the back of the sword to move the sword in a clockwise direction and blocks the thrust to the right as in Fig. 37 (Figs. 40-42).

Fig. 41

Fig. 42

Fig. 43

Fig. 44

Once more, uchikomi steps foward with the left foot and thrusts a third time at the face (Figs. 43-46).

As the third thrust comes towards the face, uketachi steps back with the right foot and blocks towards the left, keeping the tip on the centerline (Figs. 43-45).

79

Fig. 45

Fig. 46

Uketachi steps forward with the right foot while sliding the sword down the jo and cutting the waist in a semi-circular movement from high to low as in the first and second partner practice (Figs. 47-51).

Fig. 47

Uchikomi slides back, right foot then left foot, as in the first two partner practices. The tip of the jo circles clockwise with the back of the right hand touching the forehead, blocking the sword to the left (Figs. 48-51).

Fig. 48

Fig. 49

Fig. 50

Fig. 51

The uketachi raises the sword to the upper position over the head (jodan) while leaving the right leg exposed (Figs. 52, 53).

Fig. 52

Uchikomi steps forward with the right foot, dropping to the left knee while bringing the jo up over the head and striking down towards the inside of uketachi's right knee (Figs. 52-56).

Fig. 53

Fig. 54

Uketachi steps back with the right foot, toe to toe with the left foot, while cutting straight down on the left side of the jo (Figs. 54-56).

Fig. 55

Fig. 56

Uketachi then rotates the sword counter clockwise with the cutting edge facing up (Fig. 57).

Fig. 57

Uketachi steps in with the left foot and cuts down on top the head (Figs 58-60).

Fig. 58

Uchikomi steps up and to the left with the left foot, then pivots, bringing the right foot around behind (Figs. 58-61).

Fig. 59

Fig. 60

Fig. 61

Fig. 62

Fig. 63

At the same time, uchikomi withdraws the jo and brings the left hand up and over in a circular movement, striking down on the back of the sword (Figs. 58-61).

The uketachi steps to the right with the right foot while bringing the sword around the head in a large circular motion and cuts the left side of the uchikomi at waist level (Figs. 62-65).

Uchikomi steps to the right with the right foot first while pivoting the left foot around behind. At the same time, the jo is held in the right hand while the left hand slides over the right, grabbing the end of the jo and striking down on the side of the sword. It is important that both hands are on top of the jo and when the sword is contacted, the left hand is attached to the left hip (Figs. 62-66).

Fig. 64

Fig. 65

Fig. 66

Fig. 67

Fig. 68

Fig. 69

Uchikomi moves the jo from the sword to the centerline of the uketachi. When the jo releases the sword, uketachi steps back with the left foot and finishes with maki-uchi (Figs. 67-72).

Fig. 70

Fig. 71

Fig. 72

Chapter 3: Soft style Kumijo
(Sword against Jo)

Kumijo #5

Both partners stand in ura-no-seigan with weapons overlapping approximately four or five inches (Fig. 1). Uketachi has the tip of the sword at solar plexus level and the left hand touching the center (Fig. 1).

Uchikomi matches the level of the sword tip, positioning the left hand to the left of center, near the body (Fig. 1).

Fig. 1

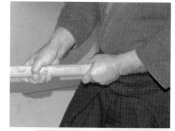

Fig. 2

Fig. 3

Both partners step up with their left foot, toe to toe, then step back with their right foot, neither gaining or losing ground (Figs. 2-6).

At the same time, the sword and jo will pivot up and to the rear, finishing in sha-no-kamae (Figs. 3-6).

Fig. 4

Fig. 5

Fig. 6

Fig. 7

Fig. 8

Fig. 9

Uketachi initiates by bringing the sword up to hidari jodan-no-kamae (Figs. 8-11).

Fig. 10

Fig. 11

Uketachi then steps
up with the right foot,
toe to toe, cutting down
to the level of ura-no-
seigan (Figs. 12-14).

Fig. 12

Fig. 13

Fig. 14

Fig. 15

Fig. 16

Fig. 17

Fig. 18

Uketachi steps forward with the right foot and cuts towards uchikomi's head with maki-uchi (Figs. 18-20).

As uketachi cuts the head, uchikomi steps back with the left foot, cutting down on the back of the sword with the jo, finishing with the tip of the jo at face level, gasshi-uchi (Figs. 19-22).

95

Fig. 19

Fig. 20

Fig. 21

Awase-uchi

Fig. 1

Fig. 2

Fig. 3

Fig. 4

Fig. 5

Fig. 6

Fig. 22

At the moment of contact, the sword will rotate 90° counter clockwise, twelve o'clock to nine o'clock, pushing the sword down (Figs. 22-24).

Fig. 23

When the jo is pushed down, uchikomi raises both hands up and over the head, stepping forward with the left foot and cutting to the right side of uketachi's head, yokomen-uchi (Figs. 23-26).

Fig. 24

Fig. 25

When the jo comes towards the head, uketachi steps back with the right foot and blocks towards the right, keeping the tip of the sword on the centerline (Figs. 24-26).

Fig. 26

When the jo is blocked, uchikomi steps back and to the right into position, ready to strike gedan-gaeshi (Figs. 26, 27).

Fig. 27

At the same time uchikomi is moving into gedan-gaeshi, uketachi pivots slightly on the right foot and drops the sword to gyaku gedan-no-kamae so the tip of the sword is on the centerline (Figs. 26, 27).

Uchikomi steps forward with the right foot striking the left knee (Figs. 28-30).

Fig. 28

Fig. 29

Uketachi steps back with the left foot and raises the arms up, circling the sword in a clockwise directon, cutting down to meet the sword (Figs. 29-31).

Fig. 30

Immediately after the block, uketachi steps forward with the right foot and cuts down on top the right wrist (Figs. 32-33).

Fig. 31

Fig. 32

Uchikomi steps back and to the right, rotating the right hand and striking down with the jo on the back of the sword (Figs. 32, 33).

Fig. 33

Fig. 34

Uchikomi then steps forward with the right foot and thrusts to the mid-section of uketachi (Figs. 34-36).

Fig. 35

Uketachi steps back with the right foot and pulls the sword towards the center, so the left hand is touching just below the belt. At the same time, uketachi makes a small V with the tip of the sword, disengaging under the jo from left to right (Figs. 34-37).

Fig. 36

From the another angle.

Fig. 37

Uketachi disengages back to the left side of the jo by making another small V from right to left, then extending the hands forward so the sword now crosses underneath the jo. Uketachi then steps forward with the right foot while lifting the jo up, going down on the left knee, and circling the sword around the head, striking the inside of the right knee (Figs. 38-42).

Fig. 38

Fig. 39

Fig. 40

Uchikomi slides or hops backwards remaining in right hanmi and striking down on the side of the sword (Figs. 40-42).

Fig. 41

Fig. 42

From the another angle.

Uchikomi steps forward with the right foot and thrusts towards uketachi's face (Figs. 42-44).

Fig. 43

Fig. 44

Uketachi moves towards the left with the right foot only, while evading uchikomi's thrust. At the same time, the sword comes up from underneath with the cutting edge up, blocking the jo (Figs. 44, 45).

Fig. 45

From the another angle.

Fig. 46

Uketachi steps forward with the left foot, bringing the sword around the head and cutting uchikomi's waist on the right side (Figs. 46-48).

Fig. 47

Uchikomi pulls the right foot back, even with the left foot, while circling the jo counter clockwise, bringing the jo from underneath to block the cut at the waist. The left hand is positioned by the left shoulder and the right hand is by the lower right ribs (Figs. 46-48).

Fig. 48

From the another angle.

Uchikomi steps back once more with the right foot and brings the jo around the head, striking uketachi in the right side of the head, yokomen-uchi (Figs. 49-51).

Fig. 49

Fig. 50

Uketachi pivots slightly on the left foot and receives the strike, being sure to extend the arms and keeping the tip of the sword on the centerline (Figs. 51, 52).

Fig. 51

107

After the jo is blocked, uchikomi recovers into tsuki-no-kamae with the left foot forward (Figs. 52-54).

Fig. 52

From the another angle.

Fig. 53

When the jo releases from the sword, uketachi steps backwards with the left foot and recovers with maki-uchi (Figs. 53, 54).

Fig. 54

Kumijo #6

Fig. 1

Fig. 2

Fig. 3

The sixth kumijo begins the same as number five, with both partners stepping up toe to toe with the left foot and back with the right, not gaining or losing distance while taking sha-no-kamae (Figs. 1-6).

Fig. 4

Fig. 5

Uketachi raises the sword to jodan, the same as number five (Figs. 7-9).

Fig. 6

Fig. 7

Uketachi steps up toe to toe and cuts down (Figs. 10-14).

Fig. 8

Fig. 9

Fig. 10

Fig. 11

Fig. 12

Fig. 13

Fig. 14

Fig. 15

Fig. 16

Fig. 17

Fig. 18

Fig. 19

Uketachi then steps forward with the right foot and cuts uchikomi's head with maki-uchi (Figs. 15-17).

Uchikomi steps back with the left foot and cuts down on the back of the sword, exactly like number five (Figs. 16-18).

At the moment of impact, uketachi turns the sword from twelve o'clock to nine o'clock as in number five (Figs. 19, 20).

Fig. 20

Fig. 21

Fig. 22

Fig. 23

Uchikomi then withdraws the jo part way so the left hand is on the top, approximately half way down the jo, and the right hand is underneath at about one quarter of the way down the jo (Figs. 19, 20).

Uchikomi enters to the left side, first with the left foot, then bringing the right foot behind and arriving in a left hanmi while striking down on the right wrist of the uketachi (Figs. 21, 22).

Without moving the feet, uketachi blocks to the right with the tip of the sword on the centerline (Figs. 20-22).

From the another angle.

Uchikomi holds the jo with the right hand while moving the jo downward in a circular fashion, sliding the left hand over the right hand and gripping the jo with both hands on top, yin style (Figs. 22-24).

Fig. 24

Fig. 25

Fig. 26

Fig. 27

At the same time, uchikomi steps to the right, first with the right foot, then pivoting the left foot behind and finishing in a right hanmi. Uchikomi delivers an over head strike to the left side of uketachi's head when the feet arrive in right hanmi (Figs. 23-25).

Uketachi does not move the feet, keeps the tip of the sword on the centerline and moves the arms from the right to the left side blocking uchikomi's strike to the head (Figs. 23-25).

From the another angle.

Uchikomi withdraws the jo, keeping both hands on top, yin style, then jumps straight up, pivoting from a right hanmi to a left hanmi while at the same time striking straight up uketachi's centerline (Figs. 25-28).

115

Fig. 28

Uketachi steps back with the right foot while making a counter clockwise cut over the top of the jo, as the jo is still rising (Figs. 26-28).

From the another angle.

Uchikomi lands with the right knee on the ground and the jo in the lower position, gedan, tip on the centerline (Figs. 29-31).

Fig. 29

Fig. 30

Fig. 31

Uketachi steps forward with the right foot and cuts maki-uchi to the top of uchikomi's head (Figs. 32-34).

Fig. 32

As uketachi steps forward, uchikomi thrusts towards the midsection, while sliding to the rear with the right foot then the left and withdrawing the jo to the rear (Figs. 33-37).

Fig. 33

Uketachi stops the maki-uchi due to the thrust at the midsection, then drops the sword to gedan after the jo withdraws (Figs. 34-37).

Fig. 34

Fig. 35

From the another angle.

117

Fig. 36

Fig. 37

Uchikomi steps up with the right foot and delivers a strike to the left side of uketachi's head, yokomen-uchi (Figs. 38-40).

Fig. 38

Fig. 39

Fig. 40

Fig. 41

Fig. 42

Fig. 43

Uketachi raises the sword up to receive the block, tip of the sword on the centerline and not moving the feet (Figs. 40, 41).

When the jo is blocked, uchikomi makes a small clockwise move from the side of the head to the solar plexus (Figs. 41-43).

When the jo releases from the sword, uketachi slides back, left foot then right, and finishes with a maki-uchi (Figs. 42-46).

119

Fig. 44

Fig. 45

Fig. 46

Kumijo #7

Fig. 1

Fig. 2

Fig. 3

Uchikomi walks forward with the left foot then the right, while uketachi matches uchikomi's steps by walking backwards, right foot then left (Figs. 1-7).

Fig. 4

Fig. 5

Fig. 6

Fig. 7

Fig. 8

After uchikomi adjusts the distance, uketachi steps back with the right foot into sha-no-kamae. At the same time, uchikomi steps back with the right foot while crossing the left hand over the right taking sha-no-kamae, with both hands on top, yin style grip (Figs. 9-11).

Fig. 9

Fig. 10

Fig. 11

123

Fig. 12

Fig. 13

Fig. 14

Fig. 15

Fig. 17

Uketachi brings the sword up to jodan, then steps up, toe to toe with the right foot while cutting down (Figs. 12-20).

Fig. 18

Fig. 19

Fig. 20

Fig. 21

Fig. 22

Uketachi steps forward with the right foot and cuts with a maki-uchi. Uchikomi remains motionless (Figs. 21-25).

Fig. 23

Fig. 24

Fig. 25

Fig. 26

Fig. 27

Fig. 28

Uketachi then
steps foward with
the left foot then
the right, thrusting
at uchikomi's chest
as the right foot
lands (Figs. 27-32).

Fig. 29

Uchikomi
walks backwards,
left foot then right
and strikes the left
side of the sword
with the jo as the
sword thrust is
coming forward
(Figs. 30-32).

Fig. 30

Fig. 31

From the another angle.

When the sword is blocked, uketachi pushes the jo to the left, then steps forward with the left foot and delivers a maki-uchi to the top of the head (Figs. 33-36).

Fig. 32

Fig. 33

Fig. 34

Uchikomi grips the jo at approximately thirds and blocks the sword at shoulder height (Figs. 34-36).

Fig. 35

Uketachi steps back a half step with the left foot, followed by a half step forward with the right and thrusts at uchikomi's midsection with the cutting edge of the sword facing sideways, towards the inside (Figs. 36-38).

Fig. 36

From the another angle.

Uchikomi pivots on the left foot and brings the right hand to the top of the forehead and blocks the sword to the right, or inside (Figs. 37, 38).

Fig. 37

Fig. 38

From the another angle.

129

Uchikomi then takes a small step with the left foot and thrusts to the face of uketachi (Figs. 39, 40).

Fig. 39

Uketachi evades the thrust by stepping to the right with the right foot and extending the sword forward at shoulder level with the tip towards the left and the wrists crossing each other (Figs. 39, 40).

Fig. 40

Uketachi pivots on the right foot and cuts the waist (Figs. 41-43).

Fig. 41

Uchikomi withdraws the jo and evades the cut, stepping with the right foot, then pivoting the left foot behind and striking down on the side of the sword (Figs. 41-44).

Fig. 42

Fig. 43

From the another angle.

Uketachi then brings the sword around the tip of the jo, stepping forward with the right foot and striking down on top of uchikomi's right wrist (Figs. 45-47).

Fig. 44

At the same time as uketachi cuts towards the wrist, uchikomi steps back and to the left, keeping the left hand on the hip while circling the right hand clockwise and striking down on the back of the sword (Figs. 45-47).

Fig. 45

From the another angle.

Fig. 46

131

Fig. 47

Fig. 48

Fig. 49

Fig. 50

Uchikomi continues to circle the jo clockwise, taking the sword around in the same direction, being sure to keep the left hand on the hip. As soon as the sword passes by uchikomi's right leg, uchikomi steps forward with the left foot then the right, throwing the sword upwards the thrusting to the midsection (Figs. 48-55).

From the another angle.

Uketachi allows uchikomi to take the sword around and takes two steps backwards as uchikomi takes two steps forward (Figs. 49-55).

When uketachi attacks uchikomi's wrist, uchikomi can counter attack uketachi's wrist by adjusting the distance with the left foot.

Fig. 51

Fig. 52

Fig. 53

As uchikomi thrusts at the midsection, uketachi cuts down in a counter clockwise motion, finishing with the right foot forward (Figs. 53-57).

Fig. 54

From the another angle.

Fig. 55

When the thrust is blocked, uchikomi withdraws the jo into sha-no-kamae with the hands on top (Figs. 57, 58).

Fig. 57

Fig. 58

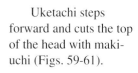

Uketachi steps forward and cuts the top of the head with maki-uchi (Figs. 59-61).

Fig. 59

Uchikomi steps back and to the right with the right foot only while coming up underneath the sword with the jo (Fig. 60). The right hand should be touching the top of the forehead with the left leg and arm fully extended.

Fig. 60

From another angle.

After the sword is blocked. uchikomi with-draws the jo into sha-no-kamae once more (Figs. 61, 62).

Fig. 61

Uketachi steps forward with the right foot, cutting once more to the top of the head with a maki-uchi (Figs. 62-64).

Fig. 62

136

Fig. 63

Uchikomi steps back and to the left with the left foot only, while coming up underneath the sword as in the previous movement, with the right leg and arm fully extended (Figs. 63, 64).

Fig. 64

Uchikomi withdraws the jo at shoulder level with both hands still on top, then steps forward, striking uketachi in the side of the head, yoko-men-uchi (Figs. 65-68).

From the another angle.

Fig. 65

137

Fig. 66

Uketachi steps back with the right foot and blocks the jo to the right, keeping the tip of the sword on the centerline (Figs. 67-69).

Fig. 67

Fig. 68

Fig. 69

Uketachi finishes by stepping back with the left foot while cutting maki-uchi, as uchikomi circles the tip of the jo around to uketachi's solar plexus (Figs. 70, 71).

Fig. 70

Fig. 71

Kumijo #8

Fig. 1

Uketachi and uchikomi both step up toe to toe with the left foot and back with the right foot, neither gaining or losing distance. At the same time, uketachi moves into sha-no-kamae and uchikomi moves into in-no-kamae (Figs. 1-5).

Fig. 2

Fig. 3

Fig. 1

Fig. 5

Uchikomi steps
forward with the right
foot and strikes the
left side of uketachi at
waist level (Figs. 6-8).

Fig.6

Fig.7

Fig.8

From the another angle.

Fig.9

Uketachi pivots on the right foot, stepping back with the left while cutting under the jo (Figs. 7, 8). With the sword under the jo, uketachi lifts the jo up and to the right, then steps in with the left foot and cuts the right side of uchikomi (Figs. 9-11).

Fig.10

As the sword cut comes towards the waist, uchikomi steps up and to the left with the left foot while extending the jo out in front at shoulder level with the tip pointing to the right (Figs.10, 11). Uchikomi then pivots on the left foot bringing the right foot behind, right hanmi, and striking the head with shomen-uchi (Figs. 12, 13).

Fig.11

Fig.12

Uketachi evades the strike by stepping to the left with the left foot, bringing the sword around in a clockwise motion and catching the jo with the back of the blade (Figs. 12, 13). Uketachi then steps forward with the right foot and thrusts at the left side of uchikomi's neck (Figs. 14, 15).

Fig.13

Fig.14

From the another angle.

Uchikomi evades the thrust by entering to the right with the right foot and extending the jo out in front at shoulder level with the tip pointing to the left (Figs. 14, 15).

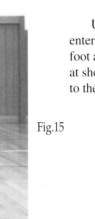

Fig.15

Uchikomi pivots on the right foot, bringing the left foot behind, right hanmi, and striking uketachi's head with shomen-uchi (Figs. 16, 17).

Fig.16

At the same time uchikomi strikes, uketachi steps to the right with the right foot, moving the sword from twelve o'clock to nine o'clock, blocking the jo with the cutting edge forward (Figs. 16, 17). Uketachi pivots on the right foot into right hanmi and strikes uchikomi's head (Figs. 18, 19).

From the another angle.

Fig.17

Fig.18

145

Fig.19

Uchikomi evades the strike by stepping up and to the left with the right foot, extending the jo up and in front, blocking the sword with the tip of the jo pointing to the right (Fig. 19). Uchikomi then steps up and to the left with the left foot, pivots into left hanmi and cuts the right side of uketachi at waist level (Figs. 20, 21).

Fig.20

Uketachi turns slightly to the right and blocks the strike with the cutting edge up, and the tip pointing down (Fig. 21).

Fig.21

146

When the jo is blocked, uchikomi changes hands and thrusts to the mid-section of uketachi (Figs. 22, 23).

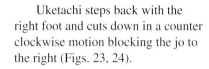
Fig.22

Uketachi steps back with the right foot and cuts down in a counter clockwise motion blocking the jo to the right (Figs. 23, 24).

Fig.23

Uketachi immediately steps forward with the right foot and cuts uchikomi's head with maki-uchi (Figs 25, 26).

Fig.24

From the another angle.

147

Fig.25

Uchikomi evades the maki-uchi by stepping up and to the right with the right foot, extending the jo to the front while bringing the hands together (Fig. 25).

Uchikomi then slides the left hand over the right to the end of the jo and strikes the left side of uketachi's head, yokomen-uchi (Figs. 26, 27).

Fig.26

Fig.27

Uketachi pivots slightly on the right foot, lining up the hanmi with uchikomi's centerline and receiving the strike with the tip of the sword on the centerline (Figs. 28, 29).

Fig.28

Fig.21

After uchikomi is blocked, the jo is brought around in a clockwise motion, finishing at uketachi's solar plexus (Figs. 30, 31).

Fig.30

When the jo releases from the sword, uketachi slides back, left foot then right, and finishes with a maki-uchi (Figs. 30, 31).

Fig.31

Chapter 4: Jo-ai (Jo against Jo)

Reishiki (Etiquette)

Fig. 1

Fig. 2

Fig. 3

Fig. 4

Fig. 5

Both partners face each other with their right foot forward and heels touching, migi hanmi (Fig. 1).

Uchikomi (right) and Uke (left) do a standing bow to each other then step forward, first left foot then right (Figs. 2-14).

Fig. 6

Fig. 7

Fig. 8

As the left foot
moves the left hand
extends the jo forward
while the right hand
slides underneath and
grips the jo about four
hand widths from the
end of the jo (Figs. 7-9).

Fig. 9

Fig. 10

When the right foot
steps, the left hand will
slide over the right
hand and grip the jo at
the end (Figs. 10-12).

Fig. 11

Fig. 12

Uke and uchikomi
adjust distance so the
weapons overlap by four or
five inches (Figs. 13,14).

Fig. 13

154

Jo-ai #1

Fig. 1

Fig. 2

Fig. 3

Fig. 4

Both partners step up with the left foot, toe to toe, and back with the right, not gaining or losing distance (Figs. 1-4).

Uke stands the jo up then sets it down in front of the left foot as in the second kumi-jo (Figs 2-4).

At the same time uchikomi slides the left hand over the right and then right hand to the end of the jo taking a thrusting posture, tsuki-no-kamae (Figs. 2-5).

Fig. 5

Fig. 6

Fig. 7

Fig. 8

Uchikomi steps forward with the left foot and thrusts to the chest of uke (Figs. 8-11).

Fig. 9

Uke evades the thrust by pivoting on the left foot moving the right foot to the left and bringing the jo up to block from left to right (Figs. 9-11).

Fig. 10

Fig. 11

At the same time as the block, Uke slides the right hand down to the end of the jo then steps forward with the left foot and thrusts to the face of uchikomi (Figs. 11,12).

Fig. 12

Uchikomi steps to the right with the right foot and extends the jo straight out at shoulder level, blocking underneath uke's jo (Fig. 12).

Fig. 13

Fig. 14

Fig. 15

Fig. 16

Uchikomi then pivots on the right foot bringing the jo around the head and striking uke on the left side of the head, yokomen-uchi (Figs 13,14).

Uke withdraws the jo and steps to the right, right foot first, then brings the left foot around behind. At the same time, the right hand will bring the jo up to block uchikomi's yokomen-uchi (Figs. 13,14).

Uchikomi steps back and to the left, withdrawing the jo, then steps forward with the left foot striking Uke's right knee, gedan-gaeshi (Figs.15-19).

Fig. 17

Fig. 18

Fig. 19

Fig. 20

Uke lets the jo slide down through the hands so the right hand is holding the end of the jo (Figs. 16,17). When uchikomi attacks the knee, uke moves to the left, stepping up with the left foot and bringing the left foot around behind. At the same time, the back of the right hand comes up to the top of the forehead and the left hand is extended forward to block the strike to the knee (Figs 18-20).

Fig. 21

Fig. 22

Fig. 23

Fig. 24

Uke raises the jo straight up and strikes straight down on Uchikomi's jo (Fig. 21). Uke steps forward with the left foot and delivers a thrust to the side of uchikomi (Figs 22,23).

Uchikomi steps back and to the right while rotating the left hand from palm down to palm up and striking down on top of uke's jo (Figs. 23,24).

As soon as the thrust is blocked, uke slides straight back, left foot then right, with both partners finishing in a thrusting posture, tsuki-no-kamae (Figs. 24-27).

Fig. 25

Fig. 26

Fig. 27

Jo-ai #2

Fig. 2-1

Both uchikomi and uke step up with the left foot, toe to toe, and back with the right foot, neither gaining nor losing distance (Figs. 1-4).

Fig. 2-2

At the same time, uchikomi slides the left hand over the right hand and the right hand to the end of the jo, finishing in tsuki-no-kamae (Figs. 1-4).

Fig. 2-3

Fig. 2-4

While uchikomi is shifting in to tsuki-no-kamae, uke slides the jo through the hands so the right hand is at the end of the jo. Uke turns the right hand over so the palm faces out and the thumb points down (Figs. 1-4).

Fig. 2-4

Fig. 2-5

Fig. 2-6

Uchikomi steps
forward with the left foot
and thrusts at uke's chest
(Figs. 2-7,2-8).

Fig. 2-7

163

Fig. 2-8

Fig. 2-9

Fig. 2-10

Fig. 2-11

Uke pivots on the left foot, moving the right foot off the line to the left, while bringing the jo up and over uchikomi's jo in a clockwise motion and continuing it down and throwing it to the left (Figs. 8-11).

Uke then steps forward with the left foot and thrusts at uchikomi's left side (Figs. 11,12).

Fig. 2-12

Fig. 2-13

Fig. 2-14

Fig. 2-15

Uchikomi steps to thr right, first with the right foot then the left, while at the same time bringing the right hand up to the top of the forehead and blocking the thrust to the left (Figs. 11-12).

Uchikomi raises the jo straight up then strikes straight down on uke's jo, being sure that the right hand is lower then the left (Figs. 13-15).

Uchikomi steps forward with the left foot and thrusts at uke's left side (Figs 15,16).

Fig. 2-16

Uke keeps the right hand on the hip while stepping to the right with the right foot and pulls the left hand toward the left blocking the thrust (Figs. 16,17).

Fig. 2-17

Uke steps forward with the left foot and thrusts at uchikomi's left side (Fig. 18).

Fig. 2-18

Uchikomi evades by hopping straight back and blocking the jo by pulling the left hand to the left in a small but quick motion (Figs. 18,19).

Fig. 2-19

Fig. 2-20

Fig. 2-21

Fig. 2-22

Fig. 2-23

When the thrust is blocked, uke hopes straight back (Figs.20-22).

Both partners finish in a left half-facing stance, hidari-hanmi, and in the thrusting posture, tsuki-no-kamae (Fig. 23).

Jo-ai #3

Fig. 3-1

Both partners step up with the left foot, toe to toe, and back with the right, not gaining or losing distance (Figs. 1-5).

Fig. 3-2

Uke stands the jo up then sets it down in front of the left foot as in the second kumi-jo (Figs. 2-6).

Fig. 3-3

At the same time Uchikomi slides the left hand over the right and then the right hand to the end of the jo taking a thrusting posture, tsuki-no-kamae (Figs. 2-3).

Fig. 3-4

Fig. 3-5

Fig. 3-6

Fig.3- 7

Fig. 3-8

Uchikomi steps forward with the left foot and thrusts at Uke's chest (Figs. 4-9).

Uke pivots on the left foot moving off the line to the left, while bringing the right hand up to the top of the forehead and blocking the thrust from underneath (Figs. 6-8).

169

Fig. 3-9

Uke then slides the jo straight up and strikes down on uchikomi's jo (Figs. 9-12).

Fig.3-10

Fig.3-11

Fig.3-12

Fig.3-13

Fig.3-14

Uke thrusts at the face of uchikomi (Figs. 13-15).

Uchikomi steps up and to the right with the right foot, raising the back of the right hand to the top of the forehead and blocking from underneath (Figs. 13-15).

Fig.3-15

Uchikomi pivots on the right foot, bringing the hands up over the head, sliding the left hand over the right and striking the left side of uke (Figs. 16-19).

Fig.3-16

171

Uke withdraws the jo while steeping to the right with the right foot, pivoting the left foot around behind, and striking down on uchikomi's jo (Figs. 16-19).

Fig. 3-17

Fig. 3-18

Fig. 3-19

Fig.3- 20

Fig. 3-21

Fig. 3-22

Uchikomi thrusts at uke's midsection (Fig. 20-25).

Uke pivots off the line by stepping back and to the left with the right foot, while at the same time raising the jo over the head to hidari jodan-no-kamae (Figs. 20-25).

173

Fig. 3-23

Fig. 3-24

Uchikomi raises the tip of the jo
to eye level (Fig. 25).

Fig. 3-25

Fig. 3-26

Fig. 3-27

Fig. 3-28

Fig. 3-29

Uke cuts down on top of uchikomi's jo, while stepping forward with the right foot and finishing with the tip of the jo on the centerline at chest level (Figs. 25-29).

Uchikomi lets the jo be hit to the right, then slides backwards, pulling the jo through the right hand and blocking uke's jo to the left (Figs. 27-29).

Uchikomi and uke then assume the basic sword posture, ken-no-kamae (Figs. 28-29).

175

Jo-ai #4

Fig. 4-1

Fig. 4-2

Fig. 4-3

Fig. 4-4

Both partners step up with the left foot, toe to toe, and back with the right, not gaining or losing distance (Figs. 1-4).

Fig.4-5

Fig. 4-6

Fig. 4-7

Fig. 4-8

Uke stands the jo up then sets it down in front of the left foot as in the second kumi-jo (Figs. 2-5).

At the same time uchikomi slides the left hand over the right and then the right hand to the end of the jo taking a thrusting posture, tsuki-no-kamae (Figs. 2-4).

Uchikomi thrusts at uke's face (Fig. 5-6).

Uke evades the thrust by pivoting on the left foot, moving the right foot to the left and bringing the jo up to block from left to right (Fig. 6).

Uchikomi thrusts at uke's ribs (Fig. 7).

Uke continues to pivot on the left foot, moving the right foot to the right and blocking the thrust to the left (Figs. 7).

Uchikomi thrusts at uke's chest (Figs. 8,9).

Fig.4-9

Uke pivots back to the left, blocking the thrust to the right (Figs. 9).

Fig. 4-10

Uchikomi thrusts a fourth time, at the ribs (Figs.10-12).

Uke switches hanmi, stepping up with the right foot and back with the left, while swinging the opposite end of the jo up to block the thrust (Figs. 10-12).

Fig. 4-11

Fig. 4-12

Fig. 4-13

Fig. 4-14

Fig. 4-15

Fig. 4-16

Uchikomi thrusts once more at uke's chest (Figs. 13,14).

Uke pivots on the right foot, moving the left foot back and to the left while blocking the thrust to the right (Figs. 13,14).

Uchikomi thrusts for a sixth time, again to Uke's chest (Fig. 15,16).

Uke again moves to the left with a small step, rotating the right hand from palm down to palm up, and striking down on uchikomi's jo (Figs.15-20).

179

Fig. 4-17

Fig. 4-18

Fig. 4-19

Fig. 4-20

Uke steps forward with the right foot and thrusts at uchikomi's chest (Figs. 21,22).

Fig. 4-21

Fig. 4-22

Uchikomi slides straight back, right foot then left and blocks the thrust to the right by keeping the right hand low and extending the left hand to the right (Fig. 21,22).

Both partners finish in a thrusting posture, tsuki-no-kamae (Fig. 23).

Fig. 4-23

Jo-ai #5

Fig. 5-1

Fig. 5-2

Fig. 5-3

Fig. 5-4

Jo-ai #5 begins the same as number 4 with both partners stepping up with the left foot, toe to toe, and back with the right, neither gaining no losing distance (Figs. 1-5).

Uke stands the jo up then sets it down in front of the left foot (Figs. 2-4).

At the same time uchikomi slides the left hand over the right and then the right hand to the end of the jo, taking tsuki-no-kamae (Figs. 2-3).

Fig. 5-5

Uchikomi thrusts at uke's face (Fig. 4,5).

Uke pivots on the left foot moving the right foot off the line to the left, while bringing the jo up to block as in the first jo-ai (Fig.5).

Fig. 5-6

Uchikomi thrusts at uke's ribs or upper leg (Figs. 5-8).

Uke pivots back towards the right and blocks down on uchikomi's jo (Figs. 6-8).

Fig.5- 7

Fig. 5-8

183

Fig. 5-9

Uchikomi brings the jo up over the head, switches hands and steps forward with the right foot, and dropping to the left knee striking uke's left knee or below, sune (Figs. 9-12).

Fig. 5-10

Fig. 5-11

Uke steps back with the left foot, keeping the right hand low and blocking the strike (Figs. 9-12).

Fig. 5-12

Fig. 5-13

Fig. 5-14

Fig. 5-15

Fig. 5-16

Uchikomi thrusts at uke's face from the kneeling position (Figs. 13-15).

Uke drops the left hand and raises the right hand, blocking the thrust to the left (Figs. 13-15).

Fig. 5-17

Fig. 5-18

Fig. 5-19

Fig. 5-20

Uchikomi thrusts once more, aiming at uke's ribs (Figs. 16-20).

Uke holds onto the jo with the right hand and rotates it clockwise, all the way over the top of uchikomi's jo, and blocks it towards the left (Figs. 17-20).

Fig. 5-21

Fig. 5-22

Fig. 5-23

Fig. 5-24

Uke then thrusts at uchikomi's face (Figs. 21,22).

Uchikomi steps forward and to the left with the right foot while bringing the tip of the jo up and deflecting the thrust up and to the right (Figs.21-22).

Uchikomi thrusts at uke's ribs (Figs. 23,24).

Uke evades the thrust by stepping to the left with the left foot, bringing the left hand to the top of the forehead and blocking the thrust from underneath (Figs. 23,24).

187

Uke brings the jo around the tip of uchikomi's jo and strikes downwards (Figs. 24-27).

Fig. 5-25

Fig. 5-26

Fig. 5-27

Uke then steps forward with the right foot and thrusts towards uchikomi's face (Figs. 28,29).

Fig. 5-28

Fig. 5-29

Fig. 5-30

Fig. 5-31

Fig. 5-32

Fig. 5-33

Uchikomi hops up and to the left while pulling the right hand towards the right and blocks the thrust (Figs. 28,29).

Both partners finish in a thrusting posture, tsuki-no-kamae (Fig. 30).

Reishiki after training

After training, you must return to etiquette. Step back with your left foot first followed by your right foot, ending with your heels together. Jo pulls back under armpit with point of jo on centerline, right hand placed on right hip with fingers pointing towards your partner, and then bow (Figs.31-33).

Part Three: Chinese Martial Arts

1. A Brief Introduction to Swordplay

Generally, the history of Chinese swordplay can be divided into two stages. First, are the years before the Tang Dynasty (A.D. 618-907) when swords were used mainly for combat, especially in the Warring States (475-221 B.C.). Second are the ages after the Tang Dynasty while swords were applied chiefly for ceremonial purposes. Because of their long history, swords have acquired an element of mystery and wonder, probably because they were formerly wielded in battles to direct troops.

After the Tang Dynasty, fine swords gradually became precious gifts. They were collected and well preserved by dignified people. Movements of swords therefore tended to become gracious, which to a great extent, exerted a tremendous influence upon the development and evolution of swordplay afterwards. The following are the two manifestations.

First, in order to protect the edges of a sword from any damage, it is accepted that the fighters should avoid using the edges to directly block an attack in combat. And, practitioners in a duel exercise should see that the swords do not make contact with each other.

Moreover, besides the outer scabbard, an inner metal scabbard with blunt edges is made. This does not reduce the antipersonnel function of the sword, for there is a gear in the crosspiece, and pressing it can get the sword out of the inner scabbard quickly and easily. Using a sword with such an inner scabbard and applying the principle of "stopping at a touch" in a contest, you can protect your sword and avoid injuring your opponent as well. But to cope with a desperate situation in a fight, you can do any effective movements whether they are artistic or not. Maybe this is the reason why a sword usually looks like a saw blade after a furious fight.

Second, the sword movements are elegantly refined. For example, attacks are mainly composed of short-range actions such as tapping and stabbing. While defensive skills are modified with spirals just like the circular techniques of the spear.

Gracefulness is not the only feature manifested in swordplay. It also underlines the movements of other weapons. Take the cudgel for instance. In spite of the prestige of "striking on a large plane" the cudgel enjoys, some famous martial experts of recent ages have put forward a new principle for its performances as "neither pointing to the sky nor sweeping over the ground", requiring a meticulous way of wielding the cudgel. This means to use a cudgel mainly with stabs and highly synthesized circles.

In this volume, I will give a comprehensive introduction of the varied sword skills with techni-

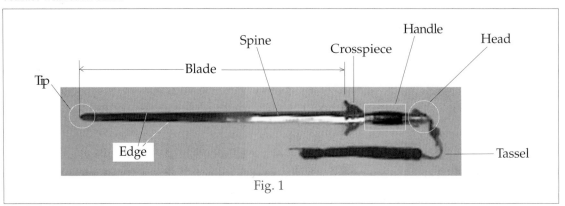

Fig. 1

Fig. 2-1

Fig. 2-2

Fig. 2-3

Fig. 2-4

Fig. 2-5

cal details.

2. Components of a Sword and Their Functions

A sword is composed of several common parts, including the blade, tip, edges, spine, crosspiece, handle, head and tassel. See Fig.1 for details.

Besides, there are still some special features due to the long history of swords and the vast territory where swords were used. I will more or less deal with some of these special features and their functions in this volume.

2.1 The Head

The head is a projection at the end of the handle.

It plays an important role in preventing the sword from slipping away from the hand. This often happens when the handle is coated with blood

Fig. 3-1   Fig. 3-2

Fig. 3-3   Fig. 3-4

Fig. 3-5   Fig. 3-6

or rain, or when a chop or a circular cut is carried out, for example.

2.2 The Handle

The handle is where you hold the sword. Two aspects of the handle should be brought to your attention.

First, is the quality and the weight of the handle. They are related to the exertion of strength and the speed of movements. Second, is the handle length.

194

Fig.4-1

Fig.4-2

Fig.4-3

Fig.4-4

Fig.4-5

Fig.4-6

Fig.4-7

A sword with a short handle is usually held with a single hand, and is called a single-handed sword.

On the contrary, a sword with a longer handle is usually held with both hands and is therefore called a double-handed sword. But what kind of sword is actually used? It depends on the swordsman's favor.

I believe, in theory, that a double-handed sword has more advantages. The length of a sword exerts less influence on the mobility but more on the power. We know from the lever principle that a shorter handle reduces the exertion of power. While you are performing a fending movement as shown in Fig.2-1~5, poor strength will inevitably put you in an obviously inferior position. However, if you hold a sword with both hands as shown in Fig.3-1~6, the situation is quite different. It is inconvenient to hold a single-handed sword with both hands.

However, a double-handed sword can be freely wielded with a single hand as well as with both hands. Fig.4-1~ demonstrates the block, uppercut, and chop with both hands. and a single one, alter-

Fig. 5-1   Fig. 5-2

Fig. 5-3   Fig. 5-4

Fig. 6-1

Fig. 6-2

Fig. 6-3

nately. Taking strength into consideration, I would point out that some prevailing movements such as blocking (Fig.5-1~4), and spinning in front of the chest (Fig.6-1~3) are dangerous and unpractical.

Fig.7 shows the way to hold a sword with a single hand, and Fig.8 exhibits the

Fig. 7

Fig. 8

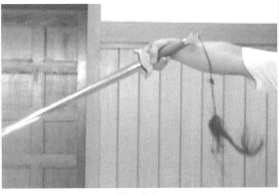

Fig. 9-1

Fig. 9-2

method to hold a sword with both hands. The sword is held with one hand more frequently. With both hands holding the sword, movements will become more difficult. It demands much, especially in body technique.

When you hold a sword with a single hand, you must make sure that you hold it tight. In recent days, some people, especially those majored in martial arts, get used to holding swords loosely in order to increase the speed of the movements.

Sometimes, the loose way of holding a sword is due to the particular actions. For instance, while performing a tap as shown in Fig.9-1~2, you must crook the hand at the wrist and tilt the handle end upward, thus forming a slack posture with only the thumb and the forefinger pinching the sword. Such an action usually results in dropping the sword the moment it hits the target. This should be brought to a beginners' attention. Be sure to ask yourself if the sword is held tight or not.

Fig. 10-1

Fig. 10-2

197

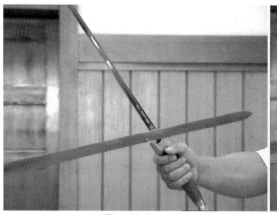

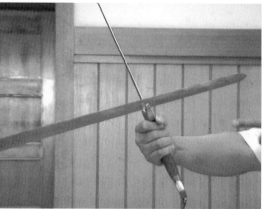

| Fig. 11-1 | Fig. 11-2 |

By the way, I should point out that some methods of holding a sword described in some sword manuals are unpractical (Fig.10-1~2). Readers should read martial arts books from the angle of study and not believe everything blindly.

Notice also, that holding a sword tightly does not mean stiffenning your arms and shoulders. If so, the sword could not be wielded in a nimble way. Keep in mind that the sword should be held tight, but the body and the limbs should be flexible.

Generally, a thick and heavy blade is related to great striking power. When facing an armored opponent, a fighter with his head, neck, face, trunk, arms and legs well protected, you could not do him any serious injury with a thin and light sword. But, too heavy a sword has a vital weak point. The great inertia will inevitably impair your flexibility, and bring about many flaws in your defensive movements. You can wield a light sword with great speed and nimbleness and make a surprise attack at your opponent. That is a great advantage.

2.3 The Crosspiece

The crosspiece is between the handle and the blade, and is also known as the hand guard. It mainly functions to protect the hand from injury that may be caused by the opponent's weapon sliding down along the blade. See Fig.11-1~2 for an example.

Odd shaped crosspieces can sometimes be seen and they usually have special functions. You should be careful if you notice an odd shaped crosspiece when you come to grips with an opponent.

2.4 The Blade

The most important part of a sword is the blade, which can be used for both attack and defense.

Fig. 12-1	Fig. 12-2

Fig. 12-3

Fig. 12-4

Fig. 12-5

Variations of skills result from lightness. A small action at the wrist can cause the tip of the sword to move a large distance. Fig.12-1~5 show the transformation from a straight stab to a horizontal caused by only a small twist of the wrist. The length of the blade also has some influence on the use of the sword.

Most people order swords according to their arms' length. But, there are some who determine the length of their swords by the features of their sword technique.

A short sword is usually thick and heavy, and should be wielded quickly and powerfully like a fist. Yet a long sword is usually thin and light. You can use a long sword more flexibly and with more changes of methods. When the blade is very short, the sword becomes a dagger.

2.5 The Edges

The edges are the sharpened sides of the blade, and are the important antipersonnel parts of a sword.

Fig. 13-1   Fig. 13-2

Fig. 13-3   Fig. 13-4   Fig. 13-5

Compared with a long knife (one side the edge and the other the back), a sword is much more convenient to use because of the two edges. For instance, if your weapon is a long knife and it meets that of the opponent's, you need to turn it over to launch an effective attack (Fig.13-1~5). But if the weapon you hold is a sword, you only need to change the angle slightly and you can injure your opponent easily (Fig.14-1~7). This may be considered as the advantage of any double-edged weapons. However, a double-edged weapon can not be used in the way that a single-edged weapon can, namely with the other hand pressing on the back of the weapon to enhance it's strength. See Fig.15-1~6 and Fig.16-1~4 for some examples.

200

Fig. 14-1

Fig. 14-2

Fig. 14-3

Fig. 14-4

Fig. 14-5

Fig. 14-6

Fig. 14-7

Fig. 15-1

Fig. 15-2

Fig. 15-3

Fig. 15-4

Fig. 15-5

Fig. 15-6

Fig. 16-1   Fig. 16-2

Fig. 16-3   Fig. 16-4

2.6 The Spine

The spine is the thickened line along the blade between the edges. It has no function but to strengthen the sword to achieve better antipersonnel results in attack, and enhance the bearing capacity of the sword in defense.

2.7 The Tip

The tip of a sword is the farthest end of the blade. It is more frequently applied in attacks than edges. The most common use of the tip is stabbing or thrusting.

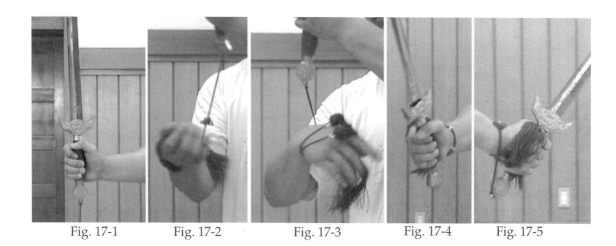

| Fig. 17-1 | Fig. 17-2 | Fig. 17-3 | Fig. 17-4 | Fig. 17-5 |

2.8 The Tassel

The tassel is the fabric tethered to the head of a sword. Its uses include the following.

First, the tassel can be twined to the wrist to connect the sword and the hand tightly in case the sword drops to the ground in a fight. See Fig.17-1~5 for details. If the sword slips from your hand, it is easier for you to grip it again when suspended from the wrist as shown in Fig.18-1~4.

Second, it is said that in ancient times the tassel was often used to clean the handle when bloody so the sword could be held tightly.

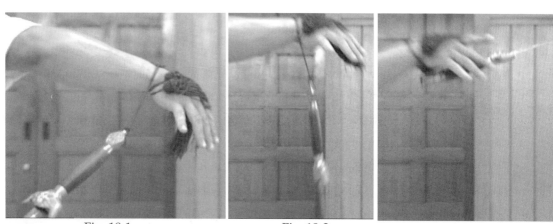

| Fig. 18-1 | Fig. 18-2 | Fig. 18-3 |

Fig. 18-4

Besides short tassels, there are swords with long tassels. It is said that a long tassel (that may be longer than the blade) could be used to interfere with the opponent's view, or even tie up the opponent's arms or legs. This is for reference only.

Fig. 19

3. Basic Attack Methods of Swordplay

Weapons (varied sorts of long or short, hard or soft weapons such as knives, swords, spears, cudgels and so on) are only extensions to human arms, just like chop sticks. Therefore, it is better for you to make a serious study of the basic fist methods first. Then, you'll get a better understanding of the weapon principles, and master the methods skillfully, whether the weapons are long or short.

As I have discussed in Volume 1, there are only two kinds of attacking fist methods: one is straight striking and the other is circular striking. As for weapons, this difference is quite clear, for weapons are hard and can not bend like an elbow. The various sword movements can also be divided into two categories. First, the sword methods of straight striking are the skills to thrust with the tip of the sword.

One typical movement of this kind is the stab (Fig.19). Second, the sword methods of circular striking include the chop (Fig.20-1~3), horizontal cut (Fig.21-1~3 and Fig.22-1~2), uppercut (Fig.23-1~4), slice, sweep and so on. They are the movements of striking from the outside to the center with the blade. However, the movement of the tap is related to the tip and the far end of the blade, so it has the features of both kinds just like a hook fist.

The sword methods are few and simple. Rudi-

Fig.20-1   Fig. 20-2   Fig. 20-3

Fig. 21-1   Fig.21-2   Fig. 21-3

mentary movements are easy to acquire, but mastery
of the arts is quite difficult. We can hold that
swordplay consists of two elements: man and sword.
The sword is dead but a man is alive. In order to
enhance your technical level, you need to study
diligently and train hard. It is necessary for beginners to keep in mind that a transformation from the
most common movements to the profound skills
could not be attained without earnest and assiduous
training.

Fig. 22-1   Fig. 22-2

Fig. 23-1   Fig. 23-2   Fig.23-3

Fig. 23-4

3.1 Tap with Sword

When you perform an action with the tip and the far end of the sword to attack your opponent as is typically shown in Fig.24, it is a tap.

The skills include downward tap, upward tap and inward tap.

3.1.1 Downward Tap

Crook your hand at the wrist and strike downward with the tip of the sword. Fig.25 shows the movement of tapping in a bow stance toward the opponent's hand. Fig.26 shows the movement of tapping toward the opponent's forearm.

The movement of a downward tap is small and quick. The tip of the sword usually hits the target

Fig. 24

before the opponent can make a response. It is therefore an efficient skill to use. If the sword hits the opponent's hand, he can no longer wield his sword effectively. If the wound is serious, he will inevitably have great difficulty holding his weapon and fall into a predicament. Just as the saying goes:

Fig. 25

Fig. 26

Fig. 27-1

Fig. 27-2

"defeat the opponent without killing him." This is a common understanding held in esteem by ancient sages of the martial marts.

3.1.2 Upward Tap

Tilt your hand at the wrist and strike upward with the tip of the sword at the opponent's hand as shown in Fig.27-1~2. An upward tap is usually used when the sword is below the opponent's weapon. For instance, when the opponent strike your sword down and then thrusts his sword straight at your chest, you can perform an upward tap at his hand as shown in Fig.28-1~5.

Fig. 28-1   Fig. 28-2

Fig. 28-3   Fig. 28-4

Fig. 28-5

Fig. 29-1   Fig. 29-2

Fig. 29-3   Fig. 29-4

3.1.3 Inward Tap

As the body dodges to the side, crook the hand at the wrist and strike inward with the tip of the sword at the opponent's hand. This kind of horizontal tapping is shown in Fig.29-1~4.

It would be better for you to dodge to the side or increase the distance between you and your opponent for safety's sake when you perform a downward tap, an upward tap or an inward tap. Some people used to wear a tortoise-shell-like cap on the wrist and the forearm in order to cope with the unpredictable tapping.

3.2 Stab with Sword

A stab is a thrusting action with force concentrated on the tip of the sword. It looks much like fist thrusting, or palm piercing.

The methods of stab include level stab, vertical stab, upward stab, downward stab, side stab, backward stab, turn-up stab and so on.

3.2.1 Level Stab and Vertical Stab

Hold the sword and thrust it at the opponent along a straight line. When the blade plane is perpendicular to the ground, it is a vertical stab

210

Fig. 30-1

Fig. 30-2

Fig, 31

(Fig.23-2). When the blade plan is parallel to the ground, it is a level stab (Fig.23-3). There is not much to choose between the two. It only depends on the individual's habit to decide which one is used in a particular situation. But from the human anatomy angle, it is easier to thrust a sword into the opponent's chest or throat with a level stab. The level stab and the vertical stab are simple. Please appreciate the methods yourself.

| Fig. 32-1 | Fig. 32-2 |

3.2.2 Upward Stab and Downward Stab

There is not much difference between the upward stab and the downward stab. The only difference is the thrusting direction. When you thrust

upward from below, it is an upward stab. When you thrust downward from above, it is a downward stab.

3.2.2.1 Stab upward in side bow stance:

As your left leg steps to the front-left to form a

| Fig. 33-1 | Fig. 33-2 |
| Fig. 33-3 | Fig. 33-4 |

Fig. 33-5   Fig.33-6

Fig. 33-7

Fig. 33-8

bow stance, you can hold the sword with your right
hand to ward off the opponent's blow. Then, thrust
the sword obliquely upward from below toward the
opponent's upper body, throat or head. See Fig.32-
1~2 for details.

3.2.2.2 Twist sword and stab upward:

When you two stand facing each other with the
swords meeting in front, you can first squat down
slightly and press the opponent's sword with your
sword. You can then retract your front leg and twist
the sword in a clockwise circle, and finally step
forward and thrust your sword obliquely upward
toward the opponent's throat or head. See Fig.33-
1~8 for details.

213

Fig. 34-1
Fig. 34-2

Fig.34-3
Fig. 34-4

Fig. 34-5

3.2.2.3 Twist sword and stab downward:

When you two stand facing each other with the swords meeting in front or when the opponent thrusts his sword toward your chest, you can first twist your sword in a clockwise circle to push the opponent's sword to the side. Then, step forward and thrust your sword toward the opponent's lower section. See Fig.34-1~5 for details.

3.2.3 Side Stab

A side stab can usually be used in a mass fight or in a close combat. For instance, if the opponent makes a horizontal cut toward your middle or lower section, you can first block the blow and twist your sword in a clockwise circle. When you have the

214

Fig. 35-1

Fig. 35-2

Fig. 35-3

Fig.35-4

Fig. 35-5

opponent under your control, you can step to the front-left with your left leg and turn your body slightly to the right, and stretch your left hand to grasp the opponent's hand that holds his sword. Then, thrust your sword to the left toward the opponent's chest, throat or head. See Fig.35-1~5 and Fig.36-1~7 for details.

Fig. 36-1

Fig. 36-2

Fig. 36-3

Fig. 36-4

Fig. 36-5

Fig. 36-6

Fig. 36-7

Fig. 37-1   Fig. 3-72

Fig. 37-3   Fig. 37-4

3.2.4 Backward Stab

Turn the tip of the sword to the rear suddenly and thrust the sword toward the opponent who attacks from the back. Such an action is called a backward stab.

Generally, a backward stab can be performed in a turn, dodge, crouch stance, cross-legged squat and so on. Fig.37-1~4 describe a typical backward stab. Fig.38-1~4 demonstrate a backward stab in a crouch stance. Such an action is usually called a sword penetrating.

Backward stab is as common as forward stab, and people usually take it for granted. But in fact, it is sometimes dangerous or unpractical. For

instance, if you perform a backward stab in a turn, crouch stance or cross-legged squat, the attack

often fails due to the long distance between you and your opponent as shown in Fig.39.

Theoretically, a backward stab in a crouch stance is an integrated action. The body's great drop makes the opponent's attack come to nothing. The stretched arm makes the sword close to the opponent.

Moreover, the performance is elegant. However, such an action is unpractical. A straight thrust is flexible and as swift as lightning, and does not possess the great inertia that a chopping fist has. So, if the opponent makes a straight thrust with his sword, he will have enough time to change his movements before you can finish your drop and backward stab. We can see this situation clearly in Fig.40-1~4. Objectively, you will have enough time to lower your body and launch a counterattack if the

Fig. 38-1   Fig. 38-2

Fig. 38-3   Fig. 38-4

opponent is performing a horizontal cut, for the inertia of the blow can't be ignored.

It is very difficult for you to judge whether the cut is toward your upper, middle or lower section. It's easier to judge the opponent's range of movements if he attacks with his fists or legs. But with a

Fig. 39

sword, the situation becomes bewildering. A small action at the wrist will swiftly change the weapon's target.

We can occasionally see the backward stab with the body turning over in drunkard boxing routines. Such a showy action is dangerous and is only suitable for exhibition.

Sharpened weapons are not the same as fists and legs. You can continue to fight even after you have been hit several times by fists or legs, but you will be seriously wounded or even meet your death if you are hit by a sword. So, we should attach primary importance to the safety of every movement.

Efficient counterattacking movements with poor safety are usually called desperate skills. You should not use them unless you are driven into a corner. It

Fig. 40-1

Fig. 40-2

Fig. 40-3

Fig. 40-4

3.2.5 Turn-up Stab

seems as if desperate skills are useless in recent days, but it is still interesting to study them.

You can counterattack with a turn-up stab when your head is threatened by a thrust as shown in Fig.41-1~4. When the opponent thrusts his sword toward your head, you can lower your body and

Fig. 41-1

Fig. 41-2

Fig. 41-3

Fig. 41-4

Fig. 42-1

Fig. 42-2

Fig. 42-3

Fig. 42-4

take a step to the front left with your left leg. Meanwhile, hold the sword with your right hand and raise it with the forearm rotating inward to ward off the oncoming attack. Then step forward with your right leg, and stab backhanded at the opponent with your sword. See Fig.42-1~4 for details. This action is the same as a turn-up fist thrust shown in Fig.43-1~5.

Fig. 43-1   Fig. 43-2   Fig. 43-3

Fig. 43-4   Fig. 43-5

Fig. 44-1   Fig. 44-2

Fig. 44-3   Fig. 44-4

3.3 Chop with Sword

A chop is an action to cut downward or obliquely downward with the blade as shown in Fig.44-1~4, Fig.45-1~4 and Fig.46-1~4. There is not much

difference between a chop with a sword and a chop with a hand.

Chopping belongs to the category of circular striking, and is an efficient movement in Japanese swordplay. Fig.47 exhibits the movement of a chop across three linked sections: sword, arm and head.

222

Fig. 45-1   Fig. 45-2

Fig. 45-3   Fig. 45-4

223

Fig. 46-1   Fig. 46-2

Fig. 46-3   Fig. 46-4

3.3.1 Block and chop:

If the opponent strikes a head-on blow, you can wield your sword to the upper-front to ward off the attack and then chop at him. Details are shown in Fig.48-1~5. Your body should move to the front-right while you conduct the chopping in case the opponent's weapon drops to wound you.

Fig. 47-1

Fig. 47-2

Fig. 47-3

Fig. 47-4

Fig. 47-5

Fig. 48-1

Fig. 48-2

Fig. 48-3   Fig. 48-4   Fig. 48-5

Fig. 49-1   Fig.49-2

Fig. 49-3   Fig. 49-4

3.3.2 Parry and chop:

If the opponent thrusts his weapon toward your lower section, you can first swing your sword downward and backward to parry the attack. Then, with your sword going in a vertical circle, upward and forward, chop at him. See Fig.49-1~4 for details.

Fig. 50-1

Fig. 50-2

Fig. 50-3

Fig. 50-4

Fig. 50-5

Fig. 50-6

Fig. 50-7

3.3.3 Twist and chop:

If the opponent thrusts his weapon straight toward your chest, you can twist your sword round his weapon in a counterclockwise circle to dispel the attack and chop at him. See Fig.50-1~7 for details. It is better for you to twist the sword with both hands, for two hands can exert greater strength and enhance the efficiency of the movement.

Fig.51-1

Fig. 51-2

Fig. 52-1

Fig. 52-2

3.4 Uppercut with Sword

The movement to cut upward with the blade is called an uppercut.

Fig.51-1~2 show an uppercut to the back, and Fig.52-1~2 show an uppercut to the front. The following are three examples.

3.4.1 Chop, uppercut and strike from side:

Take a side stance and chop with your sword to the right side of the opponent's head. When the blow is blocked, turn your body slightly to the left and move your left foot to the rear from behind the right leg. As you squat down slightly, the right leg takes a step to the rear to form a left bow stance. At the same time, swing the sword counterclockwise in a vertical plane in front of your body, making an uppercut toward the opponent's lower section. If this second attack is blocked, move your left foot to the rear from behind the right leg to form a high cross-legged stance. Then, raise the sword to strike the opponent from his left side. See Fig.53-1~12 for details.

Fig.53-1   Fig. 53-2

Fig. 53-3   Fig. 53-4

Fig. 53-5   Fig. 53-6

Fig. 53-7   Fig. 53-8

Fig. 53-9   Fig. 53-10   Fig. 53-11

Fig. 53-12

3.4.2 Front block and uppercut:

If the opponent makes an uppercut toward your lower section, you should raise your right leg with the knee bent and hold your sword in front of the body to block the attack. Then, step forward with your right leg and left leg successively and squat down slightly. Now, launch an uppercut at the opponent. See Fig.54-1~6 for details.

Fig. 54-1   Fig.54-2

Fig. 54-3   Fig. 54-4

Fig. 54-5

Fig. 54-6

Fig. 55-1

Fig. 55-2

Fig. 55-3

Fig. 55-4

Fig. 55-5

Fig. 55-6

3.4.3 Side block and uppercut in a bow stance:

If the opponent thrusts his cudgel straight toward your chest, take a step to the rear with your right leg and wield your sword to the left to ward off the blow. Then, take a step forward with your right leg to form a right bow stance and launch an uppercut at the opponent. See Fig.55-1~6 for details.

Fig. 56-1　　　　　　　　　　Fig. 56-2

Fig. 56-3

3.5 Horizontal Cut with Sword

Cutting with the blade from left to right or right to left is called a horizontal cut as shown in Fig.56-1~3 and Fig.57-1~3.

Fig. 57-1

Fig.57-2

Fig. 57-3

Fig.58-1   Fig. 58-2

Fig. 58-3

Fig. 59-1

Fig. 59-2   Fig. 59-3

Horizontal cut is the name of a group of move- ments in common use. We can find several of them in "Swordplay Routine for Competition" and "Competition Rules of Martial Arts" that are published by China Institute of Martial Arts. The movement shown in Fig.58-1~3 is called a crosscut. The movement shown in Fig.59-1~3 is called a sweep. The movement shown in Fig.60-1~5 and Fig.61-1~5 is called a slice. The movement shown in Fig.62-1~7 is called a spin. The movement

Fig. 60-1   Fig. 60-2   Fig. 60-3

Fig. 60-4   Fig. 60-5

shown in Fig.63-1~5 is called a hack. Although there are some differences in detail and application among these actions, they all belong in the category of circular striking.

The method of a horizontal cut is much like that of a horizontal punch or a hook fist. The following are some examples.

Fig. 61-1   Fig. 61-2

Fig.61-3    Fig.61-4    Fig. 61-5

Fig. 62-1   Fig. 62-2

Fig. 62-3   Fig. 62-4

Fig.62-5   Fig. 62-6

Fig. 62-7

Fig. 63-1   Fig. 63-2   Fig. 63-3

Fig. 63-4   Fig. 63-5

3.5.1 Upward block and horizontal cut:

When the opponent strikes a head-on blow, you can first wield your sword upward to block the attack, and then step forward and launch a horizontal cut at the opponent's head. See fig.64-1~7 for details.

Fig.64-1   Fig. 64-2

Fig. 64-3   Fig. 64-4

Fig. 64-5

Fig. 64-6

Fig.64-7

Fig. 65-1   Fig. 65-2

Fig. 65-3   Fig. 65-4

Fig. 65-5   Fig. 65-6

3.5.2 Horizontal cut in a dodge:

When the opponent strikes a head-on blow, you can first dodge to the side, and then launch a horizontal cut at the opponent. See fig.65-1~6 for details.

| Fig. 66-1 | Fig. 66-2 |

Fig. 66-3

Fig. 66-4

Fig. 66-5

Fig.66-6

3.5.3 Horizontal cut in a forward step:

When you face an opponent, whose body is tight, with your swords crossed in front, first wield the tip of your sword leftward, backward, rightward and forward, drawing a small horizontal circle. Then, step forward with your right leg and give the opponent a horizontal cut at the neck. See Fig.66-1~6 for details.

The key to this action is the small circle of the sword before the attack. A tense opponent would

Fig. 67-1   Fig. 67-2

Fig.67-3   Fig. 67-4

Fig. 67-5   Fig. 67-6

243

Fig. 67-7

Fig. 67-8

Fig. 67-9

Fig. 67-10

over react, physically and mentally, to any of your movements. A small circle in the reverse direction seems insignificant, but it can result in poor responses from your opponent. If the opponent hesitates even for a twinkling of an eye for not understanding your true intention and not knowing what to do, it will leave you enough time to launch a horizontal cut successfully. You might as well give it a try. It could help you get a better understanding of the skill.

3.5.4 Block in middle section and horizontal cut:

If the opponent strikes with his weapon toward your middle section, you can first wield your sword to the side to block the blow. Then, step forward and give the opponent a horizontal cut to the waist. Three examples of thiskind are shown in Fig.67-1~10, Fig.68-1~5 and Fig.69-1~6.

Fig.68-1   Fig. 68-2

Fig. 68-3   Fig. 68-4

Fig.68-5

245

Fig. 69-1   Fig. 69-2

Fig. 69-3   Fig.69-4

Fig. 69-5   Fig. 69-6

Fig. 70-1

Fig. 70-3

Fig. 70-2

Fig. 70-4

3.5.5 Horizontal cut straight ahead:

When the opponent raises his weapon for a strong attack, you can seize the interval to launch a horizontal cut straight ahead. See Fig.70-1~4 and Fig.71-1~ for details.

The above-mentioned are the most fundamental sword methods for attack. There are only two categories: straight striking with the tip of the sword to thrust and circular striking with the blade of the sword cutting. It demands assiduous study in order to know how to apply the methods successfully, how to seize an opportunity to launch an efficient counterattack, or how to perform some actions in advance to confuse your opponent, or ward off a blow.

Fig. 71-1

Fig. 71-2

Fig. 71-3

4. Basic Defense Methods of Swordplay

There are many movements that can be used for defense. I will first explain some of the basic movements, and then discuss the methods theoretically. Then, readers can get a better mastery of the skills and gain a comprehensive understanding of the defense principles of swordplay.

Fig. 72-1

Fig. 72-2

Fig. 72-3

Fig. 73-1	Fig. 73-2

Fig. 73-3

4.1 Basic Defensive Movements

4.1.1 Block a Blow Overhead with Sword

Hold the sword with the blade parallel to the ground and raise your hand overhead to block a blow. Such a movement as shown in Fig.72-1~3 is

Fig. 74-1

Fig. 74-2

Fig. 74-3

249

Fig.75-1   Fig. 75-2

Fig. 75-3   Fig. 75-4

Fig. 75-5   Fig. 75-6

called an overhead block with sword. You can
perform an overhead block to ward off a head-on
chop (Fig.73-1~3) or a thrust toward your face
(Fig.74-1~3). You should perform an overhead
block with both your hands if possible, because of

the lack of strength in a single hand block.

4.1.2 Twist with Sword

Twist your sword round the opponent's weapon
with the tip of the sword circling clockwise or

Fig. 75-7   Fig. 75-8

Fig. 75-9

counterclockwise. Such a movement as shown in Fig.75-1~13 and Fig.76-1~6 is called a twist with sword. Generally, you can twist the sword from half a circle up to three circles. You should make a soft contact with the opponent's sword and then perform a powerful twisting spirally. It is better to perform the twist with both hands. You should exert great outward strength in the end of the twist. Then, with the centrifugal force created by the twisting movement, the opponent's weapon will be flung aside.

When the opponent thrusts his sword straight ahead, you can perform a twist with your sword to dispel the threat of the attack. See Fig.77-1~8 for details.

Twisting with a sword is not an action for defense alone. The significance of a twist is to push the opponent's weapon away from the central line so that you can launch an efficient counterattack such as a chop, a thrust or a horizontal cut. Fig.78-1~8 exhibit the movements of a clockwise twist and a successive horizontal cut.

Fig. 75-10   Fig. 75-11

Fig. 75-12   Fig. 75-13

Fig. 76-1   Fig. 76-2

Fig. 76-3   Fig. 76-4

Fig. 76-5   Fig.76-6

Fig. 77-1   Fig. 77-2

Fig. 77-3   Fig. 77-4

Fig. 77-5   Fig. 77-6

Fig. 77-7   Fig. 77-8

Fig. 78-1   Fig. 78-2

Fig. 78-3   Fig. 78-4

Fig. 78-5   Fig. 78-6

Fig. 78-7   Fig. 78-8

4.1.3 Tilt with Sword

Bend the hand at the wrist to point the sword upward. Such a movement as shown in Fig.79-1~4 is called a tilt with sword. A tilt is not very powerful, so it can only be used to cope with a straight thrust and can not be applied to ward off a circular strike such as a chop, or a horizontal cut. When the opponent makes a straight thrust, you can retreat with your rear leg moving a step backward and perform a tilt with the tip of your sword pointing upward to fend off the attack. See Fig.80-1~3 for details.

Fig. 79-1   Fig. 79-2

Fig. 79-3   Fig. 79-4

Fig. 80-1   Fig. 80-2

257

Fig. 80-3

Fig. 81-1   Fig. 81-2

Fig. 81-3

4.1.4 Intercept with Sword

Intercepting is one of the most frequently used skills for defense. When you wield your sword from the middle to one side with the tip of the sword obliquely pointing upward or downward to fend off an attack, you are performing an intercept with the sword. Examples of intercepting can be seen in Fig.81-1~3, Fig.82-1~4, Fig.83-1~3 and Fig.84-1~2, And Fig.85-1~4 show the movements of intercept-

Fig. 82-1   Fig. 82-2

Fig. 82-3   Fig. 82-4

ing an attack from the back.

When you perform an intercept, you should
keep the tip of your sword on the central line. You
should try to make a counterattack before the
opponent can start another charge in case you are
driven into an awkward position of passive defense
(Fig.86-1~3).

Fig. 83-1   Fig. 83-2

Fig. 83-3

Fig. 84-1   Fig. 84-2

Fig. 85-1   Fig. 85-2

Fig. 85-3   Fig. 85-4

| Fig.86-1 | Fig. 86-2 |

Fig. 86-3

4.1.5 Swing Sword Upward

Hold your sword in front of your body and swing it upward with your elbow straightened. Such a movement as shown in Fig.87-1~4 is called an upward swing with sword. If the opponent strikes a head-on chop with his sword, swing your sword upward to fend off the attack, and then hit back. See Fig.88-1~5 for details.

Fig. 87-1

Fig. 87-2

Fig. 87-3

Fig. 87-4

Fig. 88-1

Fig. 88-2

Fig. 88-3

Fig. 88-4

Fig. 88-5

Fig. 89-1   Fig. 89-2

Fig. 89-3   Fig. 89-4

4.1.6 Thump with Sword

Hold your sword tightly to strike suddenly and
powerfully against the opponent's weapon to knock
it away from the central line. Such a movement as
shown in Fig.89-1~4 is called a thump with sword.
You should perform a thump with the near end of
the blade (the part closer to the crosspiece), as far as
possible, and press close to the opponent with the tip
of your sword. The opponent is thus driven into a
vulnerable situation. See Fig.90-1~5 and Fig.91-
1~4 for details.

264

Fig. 90-1   Fig. 90-2

Fig. 90-3   Fig. 90-4

Fig. 90-5

Fig. 91-1   Fig. 91-2

Fig. 91-3   Fig. 91-4

Fig. 92-1   Fig. 92-2

Fig. 92-3   Fig. 92-4

4.1.7 Withdraw Sword Sideways

Hold your sword with the tip pointing obliquely upward or downward and withdraw it sideways to fend off an attack. The movement shown in

Fig.92-1~4 is a left withdrawal of sword.

This movement is often used to cope with a straight strike. For instance, if the opponent gives you a straight thrust immediately after he has dispelled your attack with an intercept movement, withdraw your sword sideways to guard yourself. See Fig.93-1~4 for details.

Fig. 93-1   Fig. 93-2

Fig. 93-3   Fig. 93-4

Fig. 94-1   Fig. 94-2   Fig. 94-3

4.1.8 Hold Sword Vertically or Horizontally

There are two ways to hold a sword in a defensive posture: with the sword perpendicular to the ground (Fig.94-1~4), and with the sword parallel

to the ground (Fig.95-1~4).

The movement of holding a sword vertically is much like that of a withdrawal of the sword, namely to move the sword sideways to ward off a strike, but

268

Fig. 94-4   Fig. 94-5

Fig. 95-1   Fig. 95-2   Fig. 95-3

Fig. 95-4

the position of the sword is different. Fig.96-1~6 show the movements of holding a sword vertically to ward off a spear thrust.

The movement of holding a sword horizontally is much like that of a thump with a sword, to keep the sword crosswise in front of the body and press it downward to ward off a strike. Fig.97-1~4 just exhibit the movements of holding a sword horizontally in a backward step to deal with a sword thrust.

Fig. 96-1

Fig. 96-3

Fig. 96-4

Fig. 96-5

Fig. 96-6

Fig. 96-2

Fig. 97-1   Fig. 97-2

Fig. 97-3   Fig. 97-4

Fig. 98-1   Fig. 98-2

Fig. 98-3   Fig. 98-4

Fig. 99-1   Fig. 99-2

Fig. 99-3

Fig. 99-4

4.1.9 Raise Sword with the Tip Pointing Downward

The movement of raising a sword with the tip pointing downward is shown in Fig.98-1~4. The method of this action is much like that of an intercept movement.

For instance, if the opponent makes a feint to

Fig. 99-5

Fig. 100-1   Fig. 100-2

Fig. 100-3   Fig. 100-4   Fig. 100-5

Fig. 100-6   Fig. 100-7

4.1.10 Parry with Sword

Hold up the sword with the tip hanging down and then wield the sword with the tip going downward, backward, upward and forward, along a vertical circle beside the body to ward off a blow. Such a movement as shown in Fig.100-1~7 is called a parry with sword. When you wield the sword on the left side, it is a left parry. On the right side, it is a right parry.

The first half of the circle, namely the downward and backward movement of the sword, is only

the upper section, but actually attacks the lower part, raise your sword with the blade swing downward to fend off the blow. See Fig.99-1~5 for details.

Fig. 101-1   Fig. 101-2

Fig. 101-3   Fig. 101-4

Fig. 101-5   Fig. 101-6

Fig. 101-7

for the purpose of warding off a blow. But the second half of the circle, the upward and forward movement of the sword, can be easily changed to a chop. See fig.101-1~7 for details.

| Fig. 102-1 | Fig. 102-2 | Fig. 102-3 |

| Fig.102-4 | Fig. 102-5 | Fig. 102-6 |

| Fig. 102-7 | Fig. 102-8 | Fig. 102-9 |

4.1.11 Twist in Figure-8s

Twist your wrist so that the sword swings round the wrist in figure-8s, one vertical circle on the left side, and one vertical circle on the right side. If the tip of the sword goes downward, backward, upward and forward, it is the regular figure-8 twist (Fig.102-1~9). If the tip of the sword swings downward, forward, upward and backward, it is the reverse figure-8 twist (Fig.103-1~7). This movement should be performed evenly, and swiftly.

| Fig. 103-1 | Fig. 103-2 | Fig. 103-3 |

| Fig. 103-4 | Fig. 103-5 | Fig. 103-6 |

Fig. 103-7

It's said that twists in figure-8s were used to cope with swarming arrows in ancient times. Arrows are light and can be knocked down with swift twists of figure-8s. But weapons such as swords, long knives, spears and cudgels are too heavy for the twists.

4.2 Defense Principles of Swordplay

The attack methods of "straight striking" and "circular striking" still work when we begin to discuss defense principles of swordplay. Your defensive movement, efficient or inefficient, hinges greatly on what kind of attack you are dealing with.

Fig. 104

Fig. 105

Fig. 106-1

Fig.106-2

The defense principles of swordplay include the following six main points.

4.2.1 Block Crosswise

The first thing that we should bear in mind when we perform defensive movements is the "cross" principle. This means to block a blow crosswise. In the words of boxing texts, this principle is stated as "to fend off a straight strike with a horizontal bump, and to ward off a horizontal strike with a vertical block".

For instance, if the opponent makes a straight thrust (Fig.104), you can act on the defensive with a tap (Fig.105), a block with the sword parallel to the ground (Fig.106-1~2), or a block with the sword perpendicular to the ground (Fig.107-1~3). You can see clearly that the most effective one of the three movements is the third, the vertical block with the sword meeting the opponent's crosswise at nearly right angles.

Fig. 107-1

Fig. 107-2

Fig. 107-3

To deal with a head-on chop, the movements
with your sword nearly parallel to that of the
opponent's as shown in Fig.108-1~3 and Fig.109-
1~3 are unfavorable. It would be best for you to
raise your arm with the sword, meeting that of the
opponent's crosswise at nearly right angles as shown
in Fig.110-1~3.

278

Fig.108-1

Fig.108-2

Fig. 108-3

Fig. 109-1   Fig. 109-2   Fig. 109-3

Fig.110-1   Fig. 110-2   Fig. 110-3

Fig. 111-1

Fig. 111-2

Fig. 111-3

Fig. 112

For the same reason, it is no good using a movement with the sword nearly parallel to that of the opponent's to guard against a horizontal cut as shown in Fig.111-1~3. It would be best for you to perform a vertical block with the sword, meeting the opponent's at nearly right angles as shown in Fig.112.

Fig. 113

Fig. 114

Fig. 115

While making a block, you should comply with the "cross" principle. Fig.113, 114 and 115 are some typical movements of this kind. This principle should also be applied to the above-mentioned movements such as "holding sword horizontally or vertically", "raising sword with the tip pointing downward", "tilting with sword" ,and "blocking a blow overhead", and so on.

When the opponent makes a circular cut toward your middle or lower section from behind you, take a small step forward and swing the sword downward to block the blow. See Fig.116-1~3 for details.

What I want to emphasize hear is that you should distinguish between a true attack and a feigned one. You should seize every favorable opportunity to hit back or create a chance for a

counterattack, while performing a block.

Blocking is not the goal, but a means to guard yourself when you have no choice. If possible, you should make a direct attack, or a counterattack, but not a block. Often, the opponent's offensive is not a single movement, but a series of attacks. Successive blows are usually carried out in accordance with what defensive actions you take, they constitute a serious menace. If you choose to block the attacks passively, you are apt to fall into the snare of your opponent. However, if you make an effective counterattack at once, the opponent can not make a response and is unable to continue their attack. The same is true of boxing methods.

4.2.2 Keep Tip of Sword on Central Line

The central line here refers to the vertical line between you and your opponent, as shown in Fig.117. This principle indicates a situation in a fight of keeping the tip of your sword on the central line to constantly threaten your opponent. As long as you assume a posture with the tip of your sword on the central line above chest level, you can not only prevent him from going ahead to launch an attack, but you also put great psychological pressure on him that will impair his other actions.

You can hold the sword with both hands in such a posture, as shown in Fig.118-1~3, and Fig.119-

Fig. 116-1   Fig. 116-2

Fig. 116-3

Fig. 117

Fig. 118-1   Fig. 118-2   Fig. 118-3

1~3. You can also hold the sword with a single hand as in Fig.120-1~2, and Fig.121-1~2.

If the opponent strikes at your lower section, with the tip of your sword on the central line, you can easily cut his hand with your sword while you move your front leg backward to dodge the blow. See Fig.122-1~3 for details.

If the opponent occupies the central line, especially above the chest level, the situation is detrimental for you. It is almost impossible for you to launch a circular attack from the side under such a condition, because the opponent would make a straight thrust once your sword moves to the side. If you perform a small movement such as a tap at his wrist, it is still easy for the opponent to make a counterattack. It is the speed of your responses and movements that accounts for the success of these kind of actions.

Generally, you might as well perform a trick with your sword or your body to deceive the opponent, and wait for an opportune moment to stage a strike. This method is more safe and

Fig. 119-1   Fig. 119-2   Fig. 119-3   Fig. 120-1   Fig. 120-2   Fig. 121-1   Fig. 121-2

Fig. 122-1

Fig. 122-2

Fig. 122-3

with both hands as much as possible to strengthen the defense. Two examples are shown in Fig.123-1~2, and Fig.124-1~2.

There is a saying that describes the main point of blocking a blow: "the handle but not the tip goes". This means to use the near end of the blade to block a blow with the tip of the sword remaining on the central line. The structure of a sword is not the same as that of a knife or a cudgel, so the methods are different. Be careful to avoid wielding a sword with the tip flying like a long knife or a cudgel.

effective than other skills under such conditions.

When you perform a block, to ward off a head-on blow, you should keep the tip of your sword on the central line, too. You should hold the sword

284

Fig. 123-1   Fig. 123-2

Fig. 124-1   Fig. 124-2

Fig. 125-1   Fig. 125-2

4.2.3 Strong hands and flexible body

This means to hold the sword tight and keep a flexable body. If you keep a loose hold of the sword, you are unable to exert great strength to perform a powerful attack such as a stab, or a chop. Also, you can't withstand a blow of a sword, a knife, a spear or a cudgel effectively.

If your body is stiff, you can not apply body methods skillfully in a fight. Therefore, a high technical level will be just within sight, but beyond your reach.

Fig. 126-1   Fig. 126-2

Fig. 127-1

Fig. 127-2

Fig. 127-3

For instance, if you hold your sword loosely, and raise it overhead to block a chop, you are apt to be cut on your arm or head for not being able to withstand the strength of your opponent's blow. This awkward situation can be seen in Fig.125-1~2.

The same thing happens when you raise the sword to block a horizontal cut with a loose hold on the handle, as shown in Fig.126-1~2.

When you perform a tilt movement with your sword to fend off the opponent's thrust, your sword may be knocked away by the opponent's weapon if you can not hold the handle tight. See Fig.127-1~3 for details.

On the other hand, if you can not make a harmonious body turn with the sword, when you

Fig. 128-1 Fig. 128-2

Fig. 128-3

Fig. 128-4

hold the sword to block a blow, the strength and effect of the movement will be bad. If your body does not turn slightly to the side when you perform a parry with the sword, the parry may fail and the opponent may hit your body.

4.2.4 Change Position to Counterattack

People usually stress defense while fighting with swords, because swords are sharpened weapons. It's not easy to find a good chance to launch an attack, because people always guard the central line. So, sometimes change your position to carry out a counterattack directly without doing a defensive movement first. That may give you a good opportunity to defeat the opponent in a twinkling of an eye.

But, those kind of movements are more dangerous, and those who can not vary their body positions swiftly should be careful when using them. I will give four examples to explain this principle.

4.2.4.1 Raise wrist to tap back:

When the opponent taps at your wrist with his sword, raise your wrist to avoid the cut. Simultaneously, tap back with the tip, or the far end of the blade, at the opponent's forearm. See Fig.128-1~4 for details.

Fig. 129-1   Fig. 129-2

Fig. 129-3   Fig.129-4

4.2.4.2 Sway head and cut back:

When the opponent launches a horizontal cut toward your neck, squat down quickly, and sway your head to dodge the blow. Then, step forward and wield your sword from left to right cutting back at the opponent's chest, belly or legs. See Fig.129-1~5 for details.

Fig. 129-5

Fig. 130-1   Fig. 130-2

Fig. 130-3   Fig. 130-4

4.2.4.3 Pull belly in and cut back:

When the opponent strikes with a horizontal cut toward your middle section, retract your front leg slightly and pull your belly in to avoid the blow. At the same time, stretch your sword out cutting back at the opponent's arm. See Fig.130-1~4 for details.

Fig. 131-1   Fig. 131-2

Fig. 131-3   Fig. 131-4   Fig. 131-5

Fig. 132-1   Fig. 132-2   Fig. 132-3

Fig. 133-1   Fig. 133-2

Fig. 133-3   Fig.133-4

4.2.4.4 Turn to the side and thrust back:

Stand with the left leg in front, and both hands holding the sword. When the opponent attacks with a chop or thrust toward your upper section or arms, turn to the right and take a step backward with the right leg while you wield your sword to block the blow. Then step to the side with your left leg toward the back of the opponent and thrust the sword at him. See Fig.131-1~5, Fig.132-1~3, and Fig.133-1~4 for details.

Fig. 134-1   Fig. 134-2

Fig. 134-3   Fig. 134-4

Fig. 134-5   Fig. 134-6

Fig. 135-1   Fig. 135-2

Fig. 135-3   Fig. 135-4

Fig. 135-5

4.2.4.5 Retract and chop back:

When the opponent gives a backhanded horizontal slice toward your middle section, retract your
right leg to the rear and raise the sword with the tip
pointing downward to ward off the blow. If the
opponent makes another horizontal slice, step
forward with the right leg, and wield the sword to
chop at the opponent's arm. See Fig.134-1~6 for
details.

The opponent usually makes one strike after

Fig.136

Fig. 137

Fig. 138

Fig. 139

another. The follow-up strikes often come out naturally without conscious consideration. So, it is necessary for you to perform another defensive movement after you have carried out a counterattack. For instance, the opponent may perform a horizontal cut after he has performed a tap. So, you might as well perform the movement of "holding the sword with the tip pointing upward" to fend off the strike after you have finished the movement of "tapping back". See Fig.135-1~5 for details.

4.2.5 Keep a Safe Distance

Swords are sharpened weapons. A body without the safeguard of armor can't withstand a sword strike. A cut by a sword may cause the body to shed

blood, or even meet its end. Moreover, in an actual combat, the dazzling movements of swords are swift, and not every one of them can be successfully blocked, as demonstrated in this book. In fact, it is difficult for you to make correct judgements on all the swift mixtures of true and false attacking movements. There is much possibility of your misjudging them.. If such a misjudgment occurs, you are liable to be wounded. Therefore, if you face an opponent who attacks rashly and desperately, you might as well keep a safe distance. A distance about the length of a sword plus an arm's length is good, to protect yourself from being hurt by their random strikes. However, you should not stand too far away from the opponent, he may feel it's impossible to cross the wide space between you two, and stop attack. The more favorable distance is a space that makes the opponent feel he can reach you with only another small step, or with only a little more effort.

See to it that you keep a safe distance that ensures an easy counterattack. There are flaws in rash and desperate movements. So, a good strategy of combat is to wait for a flaw, and hit back.

4.2.6 Cut Arm on Blocking a Sword

As I explained before, a sword should be an extension of your arm. Conversely, the arm is the root of the sword. We can regard the arm as the same thing as a sword when we act on the defensive. Now that we can block a strike with the blade, meeting that of the opponent's, we can block a strike with the blade directly cutting at the root, the opponent's arm that holds the sword. This can be regarded as one way of transforming a passive defense into a positive attack. This principle can be applied to many defensive movements such as blocking, intercepting and so on. Fig.136, 137, 138 and 139 are four examples.

This method is very simple, but it can achieve a high rate of success. When you act on the defensive, you should apply this principle as much as possible. However, while you are launching an attack, you should be careful to avoid being cut on the arm by your opponent. As the saying goes: "think thrice before you act". This means to reckon in advance what kinds of defensive movements the opponent may take. If you think ahead, you can change your movements in time to deal with what occurs. But if your anticipation differ greatly from the facts, your attack may fail the moment it is begun. As the saying goes: "win or fail only in a twinkling". I once wrote these words on the wall of my training hall at home, and as a result my quickness increased during that period of time.

Now, I have given a concise explanation of the sword, the basic attack-defense movements and methods of swordplay in Chinese martial arts from the angle of "straight striking" and "circular striking".

There are many kinds of swords, and they differ greatly in hardness and weight. Some are thin and light, but some are thick and heavy. Some are long, yet some are short. Although differences in these aspects have brought about considerable discrepancy in skills, the basic methods stay much the same. As long as you get a profound understanding of the "straight striking" and "circular striking" methods, you can use various swords with enough agility.

It is recommended that you do sword exercises with a partner, and use a training sword that is less dangerous. You should study every method and main point deeply. If you get the true understanding of the principles through your own experience, you will come up to a high technical level. Your body movements will become more and more steady, proficient, harmonious, and gracious. Be careful to avoid practicing unrealistic fantasy without tests. Indiscriminate body movements and showy sword skills are unpractical for real combats.

My original plan was to introduce leg techniques in this volume, but I apologize for being unable to fulfill it, because of the limited space. So, I intend to give more space to leg techniques and ground skills when we evolve the movements of Chinese martial arts into those of Japanese aikido in Volume 3.

(The end)

Appendix

Ancient furnace and iron smelting

1. Introduction to the Japanese Sword

The curved Japanese sword (tachi style) was established in mid Heian era. Before that, the straight one-sided blade, double-sided blade, and only tip double-sided blade existed. These swords were mostly influenced by Chinese style, but the Chinese style was influenced from the south by India, Malay, and from the west by Persia and Turkey, as well as being strongly influenced by the northern horse-riding people. Therefore the Japanese sword was influenced indirectly by many different country styles before it was established.

Illusst. 1-1. Upper: Uchigatana style sword. Lower: Tachi style Mogusa sword, made by Taira Sugawara, swordsmith, Iwate Prefecture.

Sword style and names were changed in each era, Tachi (long straight sword), Tachi (tsuka-zori, koshi-zori), Tachi (yoko-gatana, side-holstered), and Uchigatana (generic curved sword, torii-zori). However, I would like to explain about the quality of the sword, not only the shape.

In the history of the Japanese sword, the steel quality from the Heian era to the Kamakura era was best. After that, there was a remarkable decrease in quality continuing to our current time. This is the reason for the writing of this script. Eventually, for the martial artist who uses the sword, why this quality decreased and why we cannot reproduce the ancient quality is an ongoing question. I would like to try to solve this mystery in this section.

When the Japanese sword attributes were first decided, swordsmiths smelted the iron and structured the shape for the Japanese sword himself. He would do both. Therefore, the swordsmith knew about the quality of the iron. But, as the demand for swords increased, the process went to a form of mass production.

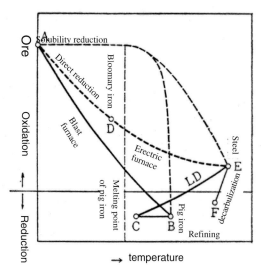

Illust. 1-2. Comparison with smelting routs by the relationship between temperature and process

Therefore, the iron smelting and sword forging were separated. Worse yet, iron smelting was changed from a direct production to a form of indirect production (See Illust. 1-2). The consistent system was broken, and because of that the steel quality decreased. This is the reason for the change in quality. Especially from the end of the Muromachi era, when the use of guns in warfare was popularized. Swordsmiths transferred their attention to the making of guns. Perhaps this is another reason for the decrease in quality. But I think, the big reason was that the technique of the swordsmith was secret and not shared among the other participants of the mass production.

Because of this situation, the Japanese sword production was compartmentalized as follows: swords of mid Heian era until the end of the Muromachi era were called Koto (meaning 'old sword'), Swords from the end

298

of the Muromachi era until the Edo Bakumatsu (after Admiral Perry came to Japan in 1853) were called Shinto (meaning 'new sword'), Swords made after Edo Bakumatsu are called Shin-shinto (meaning 'new new sword'). Current swords are called Gendaito (meaning 'modern sword'). And before the mid Heian era, the swords are called Jo-Koto (meaning older than Koto). The best quality was found in the Koto sword. (About the chronicles, see Aikido and Chinese Martial Arts Volume One, page 28.)

In the Jo-Koto category, the swords include; swords brought from China, iron material bought from the continent and made in Japan, and iron smelted and made into Japanese sword. Therefore, the sword-making process of this time is not clear. It is clear that some Chinese swordsmiths who immigrated to Japan strongly influenced the Japanese sword. But we can find that India as well as Malaysia also influenced the Japanese sword, and through Sakhalin (an island off the east coast of Siberia) and the Kuril Islands (the chain of islands between north Hokkaido and the Kamchatka Peninsula), northern peoples immigrated to Japan and influenced the Japanese sword.

About these foreign techniques, when, who, where from, and to whom they were transferred, there is no record. Ancient situations are very difficult to understand and know. But, if we separate the different techniques, one being from the southern culture, which moved to the north through Kyushu island, and the other being from the northern culture, which moved to the south through Hokkaido to Northern-northeast Japan, it starts to make sense. The southern sword is long and straight, while the northern sword is curved and short. Both of these cultures were mixed from the 11th century to the 12th century when the (northeast) Fujiwara family, and the Minamoto family were feuding. After the Fujiwara family was defeated, the northern and southern culture were mixed. The northern swordsmiths became prisoners of war and were forced to consent to move to the west. These swordsmiths were named Fushu-kaji (meaning 'prisoner swordsmiths'). The places where these swordsmiths moved to became very famous Japanese sword producing places.

In the ancient southern culture's techniques, the

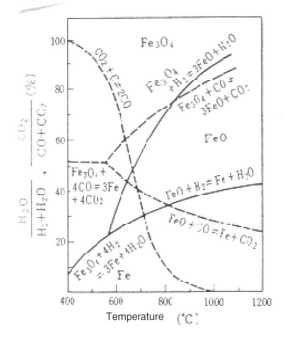

Illust. 1-3. Equilibrium of Fe-O-H and Fe-O-C

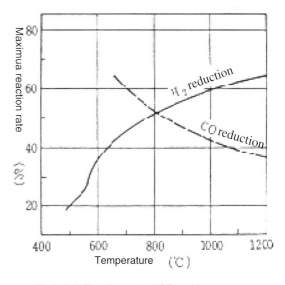

Illust. 1-4. Reaction rate of CO and H2 gas

299

swordsmiths level was perhaps very low, so there is almost no record of their techniques. Therefore, the remaining current sword-making techniques include northern and southern cultures.

In regard to quality, especially the Jo-Koto and Koto, its not clear what kind of material was used (?iron powder, iron stone, red ochre or limonite, and so on?), and what kind of furnace was used, as well as what kind of fire-making techniques were used. From this situation, I hope to try to make clear the information I researched and collected with the international (martial art) cultural from foreign countries. Also, I will try to explain how the ancient Japanese iron was smelted. The following script was published in Token-Bijutsu (The Journal of Swords) in Japan.

2. Some questions about the Japanese sword

In general, most people believe that Japanese swords were made from iron sand. In Japan, if a sword is not made from iron sand, sometimes it can't be registered as a legal (true Japanese sword). It is also believed, in general, that Koto quality swords can't be manufactured from rock iron. I also question whether Koto quality steal, using the Tatara furnace, used only sand iron. So, whether Japanese swords were made from sand iron or rock iron is vague. It leaves us in a dilemma of not going the true answer. Accordingly, everyone has questions about the materials used, and the smelting method.

Current industrial steel, that is mass produced, uses a blast furnace and is done in two stages, the pig iron stage and the steel iron stage. Ancient smelting was done in the direct method (one stage). Current examples of direct method (these furnaces are not blast furnace method) include the Retort method, from Sweden, which uses coke, and the shaft furnace, in America, Canada, and Germany, which uses natural gas. Also, is the fluidized bed process used in Venezuela, utilizes helium or natural gas. Other fuels used in rotary kilns include coal, and dust. And some furnaces are powered by electricity.

The direct methods of smelting iron tend to be more friendly to the environment than the current industrial methods. Therefore a study of ancient smelting technique is warranted not only to learn about Japanese swords, but perhaps to help the environment.

3. The development of the smelting furnace

The first smelting furnaces were the earthen vessel and pit-like ones. These furnaces were also used to smelt or refine gold, silver, and copper. Temperatures in these furnaces were adjusted by blowing air into them through a long bamboo tube. These methods are still in use today. Some people believe that smelting in an earthen vessel using the heat resist method did not produce high enough temperatures for iron, but I believe this needs further consideration.

History is broken down chronologically into stone age, copper age, iron age based on the predominate materials used in these eras, but I propose that iron smelting techniques were used as far back as the copper age. In the stone age, earthen vessels and pottery were produced. In the copper age also, iron smelting techniques were available. This points strongly at a parallel development between the two, and evidence that iron smelting was possibly taking place in the copper era.

Earthen vessels were also used in the Philippines as far back as B.C. 500 (see photos). In the Philippines, gold, silver, copper, and iron etc. were smelted in earthen vessels. The smelters were also pottery makers. Common themes in their art and pottery include the triangle and the spiral. These themes are also common in the art of the Jomon culture of Japan, as well as the Yangshao culture of China.

Chinese pottery goes back to the Yangshao period 2200B.C.-1650B.C. It was the older of the two stone age cultures in Northern China. The period was named after Yangshao village, where the archeological finds were made. In this period two methods of production were discovered, the oxidization method, and the reduction method. Potters were able to bake their wares in hillside kilns that had very even temperatures. They made some pottery that was as thin as 1-3 ml, and applied glazes as well.

China ware (porcelain) dates back to the Shang era B.C.16C-B.C.11C. The glazes of these wares contained iron, some as much as 90%.

In China, there is the example of the Daye Mine where one meter underground they have found 400,000 tons of slag. Of this slag 50% is iron, and is estimated that 40,000 tons of copper and bronze were produced. This mine dates to the middle of the Warrior period B.C.475-B.C.221. In this the middle of this period also 800,000 tons of iron was made. The Chinese developed a shaft furnace for this mass production. These ancient shaft furnaces would later influence the modern blast furnace. Chinese Chaogangfa (puddling method) which decarbonized the iron using air to burn the carbon away, included pig iron. This method began in the early Han era B.C. 206-A.D. 24.

Before the middle of the Warrior period in China, they made only copper and alloys such as tin, zinc, bronze, and brass. The scarcity of bronze can be appreciated when you look at money. More wealthy country used bronze money while poorer ones used iron money. There was some use for the easy rusting iron though, that was weapons for fighting. There was not enough bronze produced to make many weapons, but iron was more plentiful. Later high quality carbon steel was developed.

The pit-like furnace which uses moistened clay increased the quality of the product over the earthen vessel method, but the life span of the clay pit was only 2 hours. Recently in Finland, archaeological researchers from Turku University have tested ancient smelting techniques of pit-like furnace.

Also recently an article in a Finnish newspaper about the Saameraiset (northern shamanistic peoples) reported that a man, Heimo Roselli, could produce hypereutectoid carbon steel of very high quality. In the same article a professor of metallurgy in Finland, stated that the smith used a special heat treatment to produce this very high carbon steel. Therefore, the direct method also developed in ancient Finland. I believe that he uses a boxlike, or shaft furnace.

The box type furnace excavated in Japan, is similar to the pit-like furnace. To increase production, they were built using rock and stone, and were placed in places with good wind flow. Later this developed into the shaft furnace.

The ancient Tatara furnace of Japan, which is made using clay, seems to be a kind of box furnace. For instance, I watched box style furnaces being excavated in Finland, and Korea. The Korean furnace was bigger measuring about 2 meters, or the size of a tatami. This is also a size similar to a human grave. In Finland their may be a relationship between the box style furnace and human grave, because coffins there had hematite (red sand iron) lining the bottom. This is a color in Finnish shamanism that wards off devils. So, maybe the size of the furnace is similar to the size of the Korean furnace. The Finnish box furnace uses limonite which is taken from the bottom of lakes, or hematite both of which are sand irons.

According to the above chart, it seems that the sponge iron method was used north of the line, while the puddling method was used to the south. Therefore the pit-like furnace, which uses temperatures of only 1100 degrees centigrade in low temperature reduction, could be considered a sponge iron method. But, this is only my theory.

Sponge iron is a porous metal which was made from local iron, or iron sand at a temperature of 1000-1100 degrees centigrade. It had a low melting point and was smelted using charcoal oxidized with carbon and water at low reduction temperatures. Because of this sponge iron was of a better quality than granulated iron.

The chemical make up of sponge iron is listed below.

Fe%....97.00 C%....0.85 SiO2%....0.48 S%....0.002 P%....0.01

Sponge iron can be reduced at least 2 temperature ranges, 450-500 D. Cent. and 1000-1100 D. Cent. At the lower temperature the iron melts away leaving the rock gangue behind and has a purity of about 75% iron. The higher temperature method melts the gangue and produces a higher quality steel.

In Malaysia a shaft furnace was excavated that was very similar to the Japanese Tatara furnace. It uses natural wind that enters through ten air ports to smelt rock iron.

See the distribution chart of the sponge iron, and puddling method in the early Han era in China. This chart is from Hideya Okada who works for Japan's largest steel manufacturing company.

4. The materials of the Japanese sword

In 1933, in Shimane Prefecture, an ancient style Tatara furnace was recovered and used by the Japanese Art Sword Association to produce sword quality steel out of mountain sand iron, Masa-Satetsu. The furnace type was Yasukuni Tatara. But, the quality of the steel that was produced from this furnace was determined to be of poor quality by sword smiths who worked it. These Yasukuni Tatara, it is believed, were used in world war I. Masa-Satetsu, sand iron, has a high percentage of magnetite which contains only 2-5 % iron. It is because of poor quality materials, or poor smelting techniques that led to the poor steel in their endeavor.

We question whether the current Masa-Satetsu is similar to that of ancient times? For instance, ancient mining method called Kanna-Nagashi cannot be used because it is bad for the environment. The current method is a floating dressing method that is better for the environment, but may not have a perfectly matched end product. The ingredients of sand iron, Masa-Satetsu, is below.

(Natural sand iron)

T.Fe....3.46	FeO....0.91	Fe_2O_3....3.99	SiO_2....68.32	MnO....0.10
P....0.026	S....0.002	Ni....0.01	Cr_2O_3.... 0.01	CaO....2.26
MgO....0.86	V_2O_5....0.03	CO.... ----	Cu.... <0.01	Al_2O_3....17.26
Sn....0.001	TiO_2.... 0.42	Zn....0.006	As....0.002	Pb....5.0
Cd....<0.001				

(Dressed sand iron)

T.Fe.... 60.43	FeO.... 22.03	Fe_2O_3....61.90	SiO_2....7.68	MnO....0.27
P....0.080	S....0.021	Ni....0.02	Cr_2O_3....0.04	CaO....0.90

MgO....0.37	V_2O_5....0.30	CO.... --	Cu....<0.01	Al_2O_3....2.38
Sn....0.001	TiO_2....0.93	Zn....0.014	As....0.003	Pb....6.4
Cd....<0.001				

According to professor Kuniichi Tawara, in the Tatara furnace, Masa-Satetsu is smelted by the Kera-Oshi-Ho. And, Akome-Satetsu is smelted by the Zuku-Oshi-Ho. The Kera-Oshi-Ho was made up of magnetite, and the Zuku-Oshi-Ho was made up of magnetite, hematite, and titanium alloy.

For instance these material's ingredients follows;

	T.Fe	$Fe{\cdot}OFe_3O_4$	Fe_2O_3	TiO_2
Magnetite	72.46	31.03	68.97	
Titanium iron	36.80	47.38		52.66
Hematite	69.94		100.0	

Therefore, the Tatara furnace had two methods of smelting which depended upon the proportion of magnetite, hematite, and titanium in the material to be used.

Kera-Oshi-Ho makes Kera, and Zuku-Oshi-Ho made Zuku. Kera means Iron Bear in Japanese, and produced a steel with a carbon content of (0.1-1.8%). It was a casting steel used for wrought iron and had a non uniform quality.

The other, Zuku, means Pig Iron. This method usually resulted in many impurities, but using the Tatara furnace, the finished product had less impurities.

Magnetite .....Kera-Oshi-Ho.....Kera

Magnetite, hematite, and titanium.....Zuku-Oshi-Ho......Zuku

What are the differences that are present between Kera-Oshi-Ho and Zuku-Oshi-Ho? From the Tatara furnace, which was excavated, we can't tell what methods were used. So, this is a Question that currently can't be answered.

The process of reduction of iron ore oxide.

❖ 570C over.......$Fe_2O_3 \rightarrow FeO_4 \rightarrow FeO \rightarrow Fe$

❖ 570 lower......$Fe_3O_4 \rightarrow Fe$

From Fe_2O_3 to Fe is the following formula.

$Fe_2O_3=2Fe+3/2O_2$ (1)

The thermal decomposition of Fe_2O_3 under 1 atm is:

$Fe_2O_3 \rightarrow Fe_3O_4$ $\alpha\tau$ 1450C

$Fe_3O_4 \rightarrow Fe$ at 2000C

$FeO \rightarrow Fe$ at 4000C and above

Therfore, in the current blast furnace, H_2, CO, C, and so on are used as the reducing agents to produce the chemical reactions during reduction. For instance the helium gas reduction formulas are as follows.

$3Fe_2O_3+H_2=2Fe_3O_4=H_2O$ (2)

$Fe_3O_4+H_2=3FeO+H_2O$ (3)

$FeO+H_2=Fe+H_2O$ (4)

Therefore,I think the Tatara furnace needed helium gas (H2), and not only charcoal (CO).

So, Zuku-Oshi-Ho, which contains hematite, should be used with limestone to produce helium gas.

We need to research how to incorporate limestone into the process to produce helium gas.

5. Modern Smelting Furnace and Refinery

The Chinese bronze furnace was very similarly structured to the modern blast furnace (first stage of furnace), rotating furnace converter (second stage of refining). The next shows the modern blast furnace (illust. 28) and the top burning Besselmer converter (current style is LD converter).

In the blast furnace, the iron stone (hematite), lime stone (carbide), and coke is mixed. The by-product of these ingredients is acetylene gas (helium gas), and by the chemical reactions with the air, also steam (7.7%), which is aerated from the heated wind (1000 degrees C) from underneath. Currently crude petroleum or natural gas are used as fuel, and with steam, can produce temperatures up to 2200~2400 degrees at the blast pipe.

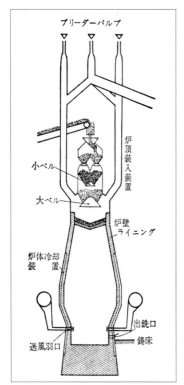

Illust. 5-1. Blast furnace

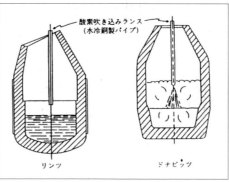

Illust. 5-2. LD-converter

Illust. 28. Modern blast furnace (22)

Illust. 29. LD-converter. (Besselmer,H.,An Autobiography, Office of Engineering, 1905(21))

Blast furnace

Usually, the rock iron is hematite or magnetic ore. The process of the reduction is follows;

(Hematite) $Fe_2O_3 \rightarrow Fe_3O_4 \rightarrow FeO \rightarrow Fe$

In the blast furnace, CO was made first, then the following actions would occur.

(Hematite) $Fe_2O_3 + 3CO \quad 2Fe + 3CO_2$

(Magnetic ore) $Fe_3O_4 + 4CO \quad 3Fe + 4CO_2$

(Fe_2O_3, Fe_3O_4 and C directly react, then became Fe.)[20]

The principle of this blast furnace by heating of the coke(C) the carbon is transfered to the limonite. Limonite generates gas by the heating. Then oxygen was brought to the acetlyne gas and high temperature can be achieved.

Oxide (O_3) in the iron stone (Fe_2O_3) evaporates, then iron (Fe) is reduced. Burning the limonite changes the silicon sand ($SiO2$), which is included in the iron stone, to the $CaSiO_3$, which is called slag. This $CaSiO_3$ covered the iron at the bottom of the furnace.[20]

Modern converter

After the first stage of the smelting with the blast furnace, pig iron icludes carbon, therefore a second refining is needed, for decreasing the carbon. Germany's Bessemer devised a top burning converter for which the pig iron including carbon is used for the fuel. In 1926, he industrialized this method. Therefore, other fuel is not put into the converter, only the pig iron which includes carbon and oxygen, either in the form of air, or pure, which was developed at a later time. This would decrease the carbon percentage. This invention was epic-making in this century. He made a great contribution to the development industrial furnace in this century, but on his first attempt his burning temperture was too low, but later he achieved success designing a furnace that can make a high temperture, adding another heating method. For this additional heating method, see the lower illustration in illust. 29. Bottom burning converter was devised. I think this is an example of high temperture being made from the blowing from the bottom.

Tatara (bellow) method experimental furnace

The experimental reproduction of the tatara method which was used in Doya iron factories (by the Sendai feudal clan) was used as one of the experience-learning exercises held at the Shiroishi middle school. At this experiment, the furnace was made as a cylinder standing furnace. The temperture got up to 1200 degrees C was made by the use of charcoal and iron was reducted from iron sand. About information concerning the sand see 3 of 5. For the metallurgical data of the chemical reaction within the furnace, see the script of Mr. Reijiro Takahashi, "Reproduction of the Doya iron works" (29).

6. The beginning era of the furnace (The Earliest Stages of the Ancient Furnace)

Xia era (BC 21C-16C), which corresponds to the Jomon era in Japan, in China bronze was already being made. This is commonly known, however this method was not created in the Xia era but was came from an older era(18). We must therefore study the more ancient time for understanding. If we compare the continental situation to Japan, the Japanese smelting culture was delayed by about 2000 years.

Smelting (casting) in the Xia era used an earthen vessel (clay pot) (Fukabachi) and the direct method of copper and tin alloy production. There were few impurities in this bronze. The ancient people of the Xia era seemed to have great knowledge of chemical properties. Further, the cast bronze included gold, silver, tin, iron. If we think about their technology, I believe it was possible for them to make steel.

In this script I will try to research about how to get the high temperature fire for smelting in the Shoko-ho (meaning 'direct method'), which was expanded from the bronze casting furnace and northern sponge-iron method (Kaimentetsu-ho).

In the case of melting metals in low temperatures (about 1000 degrees Celsius) or high temperature metals used different furnaces. If only we think about iron, its relation to iron material (iron stone, oxygen-ated iron, and iron sand), furnace (earthen vessel furnace, box-style furnace, and standing-style furnace) and acetylene gas. This is the main theme of this script.

Every country has their own history of their furnace, but they applied the chemical reaction for fire both in Kaimentetsu-ho and Shoko-ho in common sense. And I believe only Japan was without these methods.

This script will bring forward the problem at the ancient Japanese furnace, lime stone (carbonized calcium), sulfur, water, hematite (red ochre), sodium nitrate stone (potassium) were given to them not naturally, then they could achieve a high temperately fire, and need more research. I hope to introduce this mystery to the world, so more study can be done.

This research about combustion temperatures need cooperation of metallurgy, archeology, historical text research, theology, and hoplology (study of swords). This theme is too heavy for my shoulders alone, I am only a martial artist. I started my research for finding light, easy to use, flexible, not easily broken, like Chinese sword, Japanese sword.

7. The most famous steel production place in the world

Ancient people observed nature, receiving hints, to make practical techniques. This was then taught to the next generation. In the case of the bronze furnace (seen at the Beijing Historical Museum of China Exhibition) made by dojin (meaning 'copper man' of China) who watched the lava made by the high temperature of the volcano. The method was then established, I believe. These techniques included religious mysteries and migrated to other places through the land and sea routs. Metal smelting method, sword forging, and sword martial art were especially kept in deep mystery in each shamanistic religion. Therefore, there are many problems for grasping understanding.

At the archaeology, after stone age, metal smelting history is consequently bronze, iron, steel are generally thought. However, metallurgists believe oppositely having the common opinion by emphasizing Ludwig Georg Ernst Wilhelm Beck Ph.D.. (1841-1918) . Before the bronze, which copper and tin alloy was used, iron, which was made from iron stone, was everywhere on the earth. Why bronze was made first and then natural iron (meteoric iron) was used and artificial iron smelting techniques were established in delay? Gold, silver, copper, tin, and iron, were developed in the same era or not is the question. At that time, metal goods were small, if these goods were made by iron, they could not get their shape because of the oxygenation. It is very difficult to prove the metallurgists theory archaeological. I think something of our religious secrets are included.

Another point is that high quality iron was produced from iron stone in the world. But in current Japan, why is iron powder used for making swords is my question.

In Japan, current steels are mostly made with hematite (mineral stone). When hematite are smelted, manganese (feroaloy) are mixed. This proportion is adjusted to contain 0.5 percentage of manganese. However, it seems that this method was not used for iron making in Japan. Because iron or steel were made with only sand iron (This name is different in other countries. In The Philippines, black sand, In China, Tiesa or iron sand). But the straight swords which excavated from the ruin of Kofun period (the end of 3C to 7C) in Japan, I suppose these swords were made not only by sand iron but also by the rock iron (mineral stone, iron stone), because the quality were seems to be different from sand iron sword surface.

High quality mineral stone including a high percentage of manganese with no impurities is a big condition. This is what is said. The high percentage manganese mineral make high quality steel. These are good high level iron stone production places as follows [1]:

○ Calerver steel from southern Black Sea area
○ Shteiermark steel from Austria (L.D. Method)
○ Wootz steel from India
○ Brescian steel from northern Italy
○ San'in district steel in Japan
○ Gigerland steel from a branch of the Rhine river (zoringen)
○ Danemora steel from Sweden
○ Basque district steel from Spain

From this worldwide situation, the development of the Japanese modern age iron sand smelting (Tatara method) was a special growth. If we read or watch the history of the iron stone smelting using Beitetsu (magnetite) in the northeast district, in ancient Japan iron stone smelting were mainly used. This is a strong possibility. This iron smelting how to smelt these iron stones is a big question for me.

8. Special techniques for making steel

For making steel, individual techniques were developed in different parts of the world. For instance:

a) Giving carbon to the hard wrought iron, then change to steel, or from the hard pig iron take off the carbon then to changeable wrought iron. (Carbonized steel or forgeable steel)

b) Pig iron and wrought iron piled up on top of each other, then give temper by a high temperature fire, then pig iron give carbon to the wrought becoming steel. Wrought iron get carbon from the pig iron becoming steel. Both steel are amalgams to the one (Confusion steel).

c) Hard steel, soft steel make up into a bundle, and welded together (Bundle welding).

d) Make high percentage carbon steel, then this carbon (graphite) made into a ball (black lead ball-forming techniques, Wootz steel).

e) After making the high percentage carbon pig iron or similar iron material, then refine them. At that time adjusting the carbon percentage to make steel for each individual purpose[2].

If we consider these techniques as small blacksmiths, a) is technique of adjusting carbon named Katan-ho (meaning 'add carbon method') and Dattan-ho (Decarburization).

b) is Dattan-ho techniques, by multiple folding and forging techniques.

c) is from both sides of the soft steel hard steel pinches and then welding techniques.

d) is when making the steel from pig iron using earthen vessel for the Dattan, (but some people think they add carbon, not take off).

e) is at the second refining stage, adjust the carbon percentage for the different practical uses it would be needed for.

Every special technique is adjusting the carbon percentage, which was introduced to the iron when iron material was melted (from natural fuel). For instance, high quality blade for the sword needs 0.6% carbon

Illust. 8-1. Damascened sword (spearhead?) (Discovered in Rovaniemi Marikkovaara, Finland)
(Photographs are presents from Helsinki National Museum)

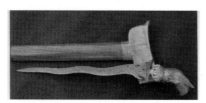

Illust. 8-2. Malaysian Kris sword (This sword style has never changed since more than a 1000 years ago)

(China), 0.7% (Japan), so after the iron is melted, the carbon must be decreased. This is Dattan-ho. If the carbon is decreased more, the material became only iron without carbon (very soft). This could be used for farming equipment. After making this soft iron, they would sell to others, then buy the charcoal which could give carbon to the iron. They use then to make iron to steel. This is Katan-ho.

About the adjustment of the carbon percentage

a) , there is a method of using air (Blown method, this is the same as in striking the metal in forging, taking off the carbon and other impurities), and adding other material (iron powder and others).

b) Folding Dattan-ho is a special characteristic in the Japanese sword. This folding requires silicon, in between the folds. This method is not only in Japan, it can also be found in China. This method required meteoric metal, but cannot take temper, because meteoric metal includes nickel.

c) Three layered iron making in Malaysia (Kuris), Syria (Damascus sword), China, Norway and Japan.

d) These Dattan techniques use earthen vessel. These techniques came from India through China to Japan.

In these kind of steel making techniques, earthen vessel method is the oldest of the above methods, so my primary research is about this method.

9. Indian Wootz steel

1) How to make Wootz steel

This method was explained by Richard Burton in his book "The Book of the Sword"(3). I'll explain by the help of my Spanish friend who translated and illustrated (lower part) some of its contents for me.

Firstly, moistened broken pig iron was put into the earthen vessel (see lower illustration) and then with small wood chips were added. Put the leaf of Asclepias Gigant or Canvolvulus Lanifolius on top of the pig iron, then cover this vessel with clay. Then the vessel is dried in the sun. After the vessel is dried, the vessel is put about twenty-four vessels into the furnace. Then the pig iron is refined with the fuel for the fire being charcoal which is mixed with cow dung for about 2 or 3 hours. After this refining process, the earthen vessel is broken and the steel is retrieved. Then temper is added again forming the steel into long strand-like formations. If a sword is made, we put this strand into a strong fire that uses a bellow, then form the shape of the sword. The sword is forged by simply striking the steel strand flattening it out so as edges can be formed for the blade.

This steel was called Wootz in India. It's called Huncluwani in Persia, adventurer Marco Polo called this Andanicul or Ondanique, and is called Alkinde in Spain. In the explanation by Richard Burton, it did

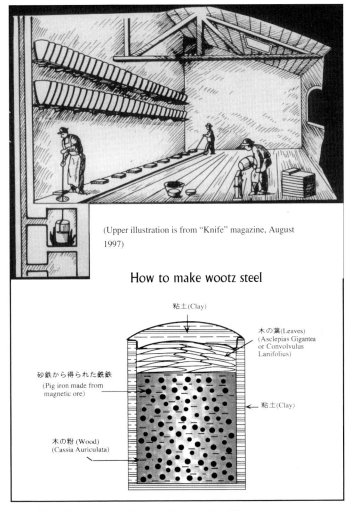

(Upper illustration is from "Knife" magazine, August 1997)

How to make wootz steel

粘土(Clay)

木の葉(Leaves)
(Asclepias Gigantea
or Convolvulus
Lanifolius)

砂鉄から得られた銑鉄
(Pig iron made from
magnetic ore)

粘土(Clay)

木の粉 (Wood)
(Cassia Auriculata)

Illust. 9-1. An example of a refining pot for Wootz

not include chemical properties of the temper fire.

Compared to this refining process, it seems to be another method for making pure iron. After several times refining for taking off the slag, iron becomes purer, and the carbon also diminished. This pure iron is used for making the sword. But it must be contain carbon to make steel, the carbon is add to the outside of the iron.

One of my students contacted to Mr. Alfred Pendray, who is considered one of the top authorities about Wootz steel in the USA, for answers to my questions.

Mr. Alfred Pendray explained that a recent excavation has found the remains an old Indian forge, complete with good clay samples from the smelter (Dates from 800-900 AD). The clay used for smelting pots was a MULLITE-type of clay. This clay does not contain silicates such as mica, etc. Rather, it was mixed with rice hulls, etc. to increase the carbon content. This clay is capable of withstanding temperatures of 1550-1600 C. The clay used to seal the top of the pot was a different type of clay.

According to Mr. Pendray, Wootz is not a *sanmai*-type steel. Rather, it is pure iron that has varying layers of hardness, with results similar to the Japanese method of putting a soft core inside a hard jacket. It has no folds, and welds.

2) Application of the Wootz steel

The application of the Wootz steel is as follows (%):
Carbon (combined) 1.333
　　　(uncombined) 0.312
Silicon (Si) 0.181
Arsenic 0.037

Iron (Fe) and others 98.092

3) Transfer routes of the Wootz method

Richard Burton explained about the routes of this method as follows:

❖ Assyria° Egypt° Asia Minor° Naharayn° Mesopptamia
❖ Egypt° Greece° All of Europe
❖ Egypt° Africa
❖ Assyria° Persia° India° Indochina° China° Japan

I believe that the techniques of the Assyrian Empire (BC 1450) were transferred from Hittite Empire Alaca Huyuk (an area within the ancient Hittite empire), which was called Alinna by more ancient people, where there were discovered ancient synthetic pig iron. This was dated to around 17th century BC. The metal made here was not iron but steel. From the Great Pyramid in Egypt, the oldest iron necklace in the world was discovered (about 3000 BC). This was made from meteoric iron (natural iron).

In the oldest capital of the world, Damascus of ancient Syria, the Damascus sword was made, which had wave-like designs (see Illust. 8-1). Very famous fighting style from ancient Kadess, which used horses with tank, originated from this area.

Techniques from India were transferred to Japan through China. The time when these techniques were transferred from India to Java (island of Indonesia) was the early Christ era, the Japanese era being the Yayoi era. However, about this time, Richard Burton had some questions, because he explained about the character of iron in every country (page 122, "The Book of the Sword"). If I use this era chart, each country is as follows (but I cannot understand if this "iron word character" is natural iron or synthetic iron. On this point I am not clear) :

Egypt.......2200-2300 BC or 4500 BC.
Assyria.....2000 BC
China ...... 2000 BC
India.........1500 BC
Greece......1000-800 BC

Therefore, before 1700 BC of the Hittite Empire, there was the "iron word character" already.

The Indian character for iron is in Sanskrit, but Sanskrit has not been decided yet if it is the oldest Indian language. This point has not been agreed upon by scholars. Therefore, perhaps in an earlier language the character for iron was included (Recently, they have found that about 4000-5000 years Indian and China were on the same level of development. Therefore, perhaps all countries at this time had a character for iron.) In Japan, Sannai-Maruyama ruins in Aomori prefecture, which era was decided to be mid-Jomon era, this corresponds to the same era of the others countries mentioned above.

The oldest iron furnace in Japan (Okuraji south ruin in Okayama Prefecture) was considered to be of sixth or seventh century AD, but the oldest swordsmith slag was found to be of early Yayoi era (BC 200-100). This iron was brought from China, which was in the shape of a flat board.

Indian Rutsubo (crucible) method was not used only for iron, but for other purposes as well. For instance, in China if make silver from alloyed silver, red copper, and lead (distilling the pure silver from a composite of silver, red copper and lead) they used this method. Put them into the crucible and then put into the furnace, and sprinkle the niter on top of the fire fuel. (This makes high temperature, but too much niter will react with the sulfur from the fuel and explode.) Then after there has been enough refining, at the bottom of the crucible, copper and lead can be found, while the silver has been separated.(16) "Put the crucible into the furnace and sprinkle the niter" means this method.

10. Iron Stone and Iron Sand

1) Shamanism and Metal

The Indian method (crucible method), which pig iron was put into the clay pot, was also used in Japan. Nowadays, it seems to not included the use of water or wood chips, but in ancient time we do not understand whether these were used or not. Adding water and wood chips is shamanism method, I believe. Eventually, fire, water, wood, metal, and earth, the five-elements, make harmonizing spirit. Fire, water, wood, and metal harmonize with the earth is very important. If this harmonizing was broken, human beings could not live in nature. This is the shamanism basic spirit.

The Shamanism spirit was transferred to Christian, Buddhism, and Taoism. In Buddhism another element was added. Ku in Japanese (meaning emptiness). Empty element was added. In the world of Buddhism, if one mastered metal, a special rank was given. In esoteric Buddhism, consciousness was added. In the Shugendo in Japan, another element was added, devil words or tengu word. If someone descended into the animal world, Shugendo would try to save this person. Like this, every religion was very different in each era and in each country. However, the Shamanism spirit was transferred to these religions, which included alchemy, martial arts, and training. This relation between iron and religion was established in India, and Chinese martial arts were introduced from India by Boddhidarma. Basic outline of theory was made. Before there was only simple training, i.e. Mongolian wrestling had no outline therefore only simple techniques, not ones that included use of body, mind, consciousness together.

In alchemy, gold, silver, copper, tin, and iron are considered the basic metals. Gold is the symbol of heaven (father). Mercury is the symbol of the earth (mother). For instance, gold stone mixed with mercury and dissolves silver, and then mercury evaporates, leaving the gold. (Gold is mercury's amalgam). This evaporated mercury becomes hard mercury in the furnace. Mercury is an amalgam easily to metal without iron, white gold, manganese, cobalt, and nickel. This alchemy was transferred from India to China. In China, Taoism studied this, and made rentan-jutsu (a kind of herbal medicine). Chinese medical science. Metal was considered as a special kind of medicine.

In the gold, silver, copper, tin, and iron, iron is the cheapest metal. Iron can be found anywhere, therefore the value of this metal was minimal. Bronze used for money, not iron. Therefore this situation is clearly understand. If a country used iron coins, the country was poor at that time. For these reasons, bronze was first smelted and used in my opinion.

Fire, which dissolves the iron, is made from the harmonizing of the elements water (H_2O), wood (C), metal (Fe, Mn, Ti, K, Cu, P, S, and so on), and earth (Si), was considered. Namely, fire is recognized as a gas. For making of the strongest fire, acetylene gas (a kind of carbonic acid gas) was designed. From the chemical reaction of the compound elements, many kinds of materials were made. For instance, in China nitrate and sulfur's chemical reaction, gun powder was founded (but in the book named "Tiangong Kaiwu", 295 pages, explained "secret of gun powder and firearms was started from the western and southern countries and later was transferred to China"). Acetylene gas was made by burning lime stone with charcoal, lime stone became carbide and then was put into water. Using high temperature with chemical reactions began from ancient times with shamanism. Metals are used reduced from metallic stones and amalgam.

Shamanism started from India and traveled to Europe and to other places, Malay islands, China, Japan, and all of Siberia. Where ancient Shamanism was popular there are smelting pots or furnaces made. In the Jomon era in Japan, Shamanism was very popularized throughout Japan, we can perhaps find its influence in the Jomon pot.

2) The Composition of Iron Stone

The ingredients of the beitetsu (Rice-cake iron)

"The height which you can see Mount Myogi in An'naka City, Gunma, the Tenjin-Bara Ruin (late Jomon era) was found, stone structures for religious service was excavated. Around these structures many kinds of stones were detected, 6 of red chert, 1 of white quartz, 1 of green stone, 3 of brown stone, and 2 of obsidian. These are religious construction and were considered for religious service against the god of Mount Myogi, because the position of its construction."[29]

One of the brown stones was called beitetsu, which was a sphere-like magnetite stone. By chemical analysis of this stone, a high percentage of iron was included as follows (page 51 of book 29):

T.Fe.....66.48%	SiO_2......4.45%	Al_2O_3...0.49%	MgO......0.09%
CaO.......0.17%	MnO.....0.15%	TiO_2....0.01%	K_2O......0.032%
P.........0.013%	S........0.005%	V.......0.001%	Cu........0.004%

"It is a special matter in the Japanese iron history that the Jomon people collected many iron stones and offered them to the god," Mr. Isamu Taguchi explained.

Beitetsu is distributed throughout Japan, which Esashi City and Kamaishi City in Iwate prefecture has a high percentage of this iron, and it has a polished surface. In Shimo-nitta Town in Gunma prefecture it has a low percentage of iron. That which was produced in Saku Town in Nagano prefecture has a high percentage but with (both Shimo-nitta and Saku) few polished surface.

I have noticed in the above analysis table Vanadium was usually included in the iron sand, but a small percentage can be found in the iron stone, as found in this table. If Vanadium was included, steel became a particular (good quality) steel, high tensile from the vanadium.

Iron Stone in the Mogusa

Mount Hakusan located Maikawa, Ichinoseki City, Iwate Prefecture is a mineral mountain, where a mine is found which magnetite deposit and limonite deposit. About 1000 years ago, a very famous swordsmith, Sanjo-kokaji-Munechika (perhaps he is of the same name of Munechika in Garima?) made swords and around this mountain there were 300 houses where a sword group lived and worked.

Documents from Showa 25 (1950) Tohoku (northeast) governmental mine department analyzed these excavated minerals. They found 2.7% Vanadium, but Showa 39 (1964), they researched again about this Vanadium and it was not detected, so it's presence was doubted. At that time, limonite was not included to the study. Because "they were controlled by the prejudice that the material of good sword steel must have only pure magnetite."(35) The recorded vanadium was 2.7%, which was one of the reasons fine swords could be made. Vanadium make good tensile steel, which were founded in Sweden. (Sweden is famous for its good steel)

The ingredients of the Limonite and the Hematite

In Finland, Jouko Pukkila, a researcher of the University of Turku, studied about the limonite. The results are in the chart below. From this chart, each chemical element, maximum to minimum is as follows:

FeO........64-39%	Fe(total).....60-37%	SiO_3........32-12%	MnO....6.9-0.1%
P_2O_5.....0.9-0.2%	S..............0.6-0.1%	Al_2O_3...8.4-2.1%	CaO.....3.0-1.5%
MgO.....1.6-0.4%	TiO_2.......0.43-0.1%	V_2O_5....0.1-0.0%	K_2O......2.2-0.6%
Na_2O.....1.6-0.4%	other.....0.18-0.11%		

It needs 1200-1300 Centigrade for melting these ingredients.(11) As the calcium is naturally mixed with the limonite (calcium is naturally in limonite), after it absorbs the carbon from the charcoal (fuel), the calcium evaporates to gas. This makes high temperature by the chemical reaction. Another element potassium (or nitrate) and sulfur also makes a chemical reaction resulting in a high temperature. Oxygen, which is needed for the burning of the gas, came from the red ochre (a kind of hematite)

Limonite has a very good quality for making high temperature in itself, and it includes manganese, titanium, vanadium, which make a particularly fine steel. This is the reason for the high quality steel of Finland and Sweden.

Iron sulfide when it was oxygenated make temperatures and naturally burns by itself (spontaneous combustion). If we add high temperature to oxygenated mineral (hematite, limonite, magnetite), the oxygen evaporates, fueling the fire more and allowing it to reach very high temperatures, about 1300 degrees Centigrade. This principle is the same as boiling water(H_2O), splitting water into its components hydrogen and oxygen. Using oxygen, it seems to be natural, but I think ancient people added their own thinking. (Ancient people understood the principle of these chemical reactions.) This thinking is commonly used in both Kaimentetsu-ho and Shoko-ho.

3) Iron Sand

The Ingredients of the Iron Sand

The chemical analysis table of the iron sand, which was taken from the Yoshida river in Yamato Town, Miyagi Prefecture used for the experiment of the reappearance of the Doya iron smelting works (17th century), is as follows:

They used a magnet to retrieve the iron sand from the river.

T.Fe........51.0%	Fe(M)......0.1%	SiO_2........9.96%	TiO_2.......9.10%	Al_2O_3......2.92%
CaO.......1.06%	MgO.......3.26%	MnO.......0.61%	Na_2O......0.14%	V...........0.43%

(29)

4) The Utilization of titanium

In iron sand, titanium was included and sometimes it would reach up to 30% titanium. Japanese swordsmiths works harder to take out titanium, therefore they never think about mixing titanium with other materials of the sword. It seems that most Japanese swordsmiths aim only at having pure iron in their swords. I have never heard the opinion that a high percentage of the manganese of the iron stone and titanium was mixed as an amalgam. However, a current company, Kobe Steel Industry, has studied and published a small pamphlet entitled "A Case of Application of Titanium Composite Metal: A Possibility of the Application to the Blade."[5]

The blade made with titanium has a high resistance to corrosion from sea water, the same as white silver. Titanium never gathers rust, as well as being considered a "no pollution metal." These characteristics are commonly known. These experiments of how to use titanium in the blade was not only currently done, but were also done in ancient times. If explained from metallurgical histology, titanium and its composites can be categorized into three systems: alpha, beta, and alpha + beta. Pure titanium is considered an alpha aspect.

Beta mixed metal is good for cold iron manufacturing. Over 90% had a character called 'extension' and solidifies into a metal with a very high strength. This is considered one of the best ones for applying to the blade. The contents of the Kobe Steel Industry's pamphlet:

1) titanium 15%, molybdenum 5%, zirconium (this is the primary metal, the others are mixed with it)

2) titanium 15%, molybdenum 5%, zirconium 3% including aluminium composite metals, (aluminium is primary metal)

3) titanium 15%, vanadium 3%, chromite 3%, tin 3%, aluminium and others are primary metals.

#3's disposition of its prescription is a better steel than stainless steel, which was used for the knife blade.

#2 titanium composite metal, did not have as good sharpness, but it held the sharpness longer.[6]

I wonder how ancient people thought about these titanium characteristics, which were included in iron sand.

5) Comparison between Iron Stone and Iron Sand

The following table shows the results of Taira Sugawara swordsmith's research, in Ichinoseki, Iwate Prefecture. He made steel from both iron sand and iron stone, separately. He fashioned a sword using both of these steels (Awase-Kitae). He folded the different layered steel 12 times, thoroughly mixing the steels.

	Iron Stone (*Beitetsu*)	Iron Sand
1. Temperature of smelting	700-1200 C	1200 C
2. Yield rate	50%	20%
3. Sword-making	short	long time
4. Temper	difficult	easy
5. Steel quality	soft	hard
6. Uniformity	not uniform	uniform
7. Forging method	hammer to expand (*sunobe*)	folding (*orikaeshi*)
8. Outer layer	(*masame*, including *mokume*)	(*itame*)
(skin)		

Note: *masame*: straight grain, *mokume*: knot, *itame*: top grain

Each swordsmith uses different techniques concerning steel. In the case of Taira Sugawara swordsmith, the pig iron was smelted from iron stone (beitetsu), and iron sand, separately. He then used the refining technique similar to Wootz mentioned earlier, and then achieving steel (*tama-hagane*). He then folded the steel. Before he could not fold, using only iron stone steel. When he used only steel made from iron stone,

Left: Taira Sugawara, swordsmith and right: Hiroshi Chubachi, sword researcher.

fissures appeared on the blade after folding. Then he mixed the two different steels, 70% iron sand steel and 30% iron stone, but now he makes sword from only stone, now without fissures appearing. (His new techniques are now secret).

On his (Sugawara) sword, *nioi, nie, kinsuji, kaen*, and *hakikake* (sword characteristics) are considered very similar to ancient Oshu (district name)-sword, appraised by Mr. Hiroshi Chubachi sword researcher. It was almost recognized that the ancient sword material used iron stone (*beitetsu*) and iron sand, not only iron sand in Tohoku district. However, we need more academic research about the ancient smelting method.

(Only Tohoku district was able to smelt iron stone)

In the 18th century when the shaft furnace was introduced to Japan from Korea, Melting iron stone were led to succeed by the Nanbu feudal clan from the district of Aomori Prefecture and the Sendai feudal clan, Miyagi Prefecture. Then established Kamaishi iron works with the help of these two clans. Therefore there are techniques which use the iron stone from ancient time.

In the case of the Tatara method, which smelted iron sand, if it exceeds 3% titanium, it needs 1400 degree C for smelting. If we look at the smelting techniques from the side of material, in ancient Japan it needed high burning temperature to smelt iron sand, iron stone, and limonite, so on, to refine into sword iron.

Illust. 10-2. *tama-hagane*, refined from the iron stone and iron sand.

Illust. 10-1, magnetite stones *(beitetsu)* (Upper white part seems to be potassium?(P) or sulfur(S))

Illust. 10-3, reappearance (copy) of Mogusa sword (Maikusa utsushi)

Illust. 10-4, Taira Sugawara swordsmith's furnace

One problem concerning the air volume, which has a causal relation to the temperature within the furnace, I think it needs experiment to compare with natural wind and *Tatara* (bellow) wind. In the case of the shaft furnace from Sri Lanka, I note natural wind method made 1500 degrees C. If high temperature about 1400 degrees C cannot be kept over a prolong period, the yield rate of the iron stone extremely decreases.

In the case of Taira Sugawara swordsmith's, the yield rate from the iron sand was only 20%. Such a low percentage was because the titanium percentage was over 3%. If we compare to the yield rate of "Mizu-hodo" such as in Shoko-ho, which was reduced from pig iron, it was near 90%, maybe high temperature over 1500 degrees C.

6) The temperature of smelting iron sand

In Japanese Tatara smelting (See, 7. Tatara furnace on page 325), this work is said that the concentrate or removal of titanium from iron sand. Some titanium is included 30%. The relationship between the titanium percentage and temperature is very delicate[8]. In Tatara iron work, how high temperature (over 1340 degrees C) get by the Tatara (bellow) and concentrate (meaning removing the titanium to make a smaller acceptable percentage) the titanium was a big theme. About this point, Mr. Toyohiko Fukuda quoted the theory of Mr. Katsura and explained it as follows[9]:

1. If using iron sand as material for smelting, watching as oxidized iron reduces, is insufficient under-standing. We must watch the iron work as titanium is removed from the iron sand. Mr. Katsura ex-plained as follows:

Iron sand (magnetite, which includes a small percentage of titanium) + charcoal

(Definition:) urubosupineru (magnetite which includes a high percentage of titanium (over 3%)) + iron (Fe)

2. The production of iron from iron sand, against a specified temperature, over the fixed value of the reduction condition (the density of CO, CO/CO_2+CO), in the case of the iron sand with a low percentage of titanium, is the same as iron sand with 0% titanium, in basic. But in the case of iron sand with over 3% titanium, titanium is mainly composed of urubosupineru (Fe_2TiO_4), and moved to the slag as a composite of magnetite (Fe_3O_4).

3. Under the condition of iron work within normal temperature from 1100-1400 degrees C, if the temperature is fixed, higher condition of the reduction can remove the titanium. For the iron production, in basic (means no titanium only iron), the condition of the reduction (CO/CO_2) of temperature such as 1100-1400 degrees C, becomes small (severely) if the temperature in the furnace becomes high.

Eventually, in the case of the material using iron sand with a high percentage of titanium, the first problem is realization of the production conditions. If using the strong wind by bellow, but the low temperature like 1200 degrees C is made. Keep the high reduction situation, that is effectively remove the titanium, and the iron production become large.

4. The slag crystallization, the melting point of the urubosupineru (Fe_2TiO_4) is 1450 degrees C, but the iron peridot (kind of stone) is 1205 degrees C. Therefore, if attain the high temperature situation in the furnace, such as 1400 degrees C, heavy iron including carbon, goes down into the slag, then produce a big iron ingot. In this case, the calcium, aluminum, potassium, which includes charcoal, moved to the slag with the part of the furnace material. These materials make the melting point low, and the slag melting situation to high, and separate the iron slag from the iron. In this material, special work of the potassium is very important.

Consequently, if the theme was the production of the iron production in the furnace the temperature condition desirable over 1450 degrees C, this has a inconsistent condition against #3. Therefore, Tatara iron work needs progress how to make strong wind for getting high temperature. Therefore, Tatara iron work is matching the bellows. Sometimes we can find shells (seashells) or other special materials which was found in the ruins of the all of Kanto area. These are called special secret medicine additions, such as including materials for decreasing the melting point, Mr. Katsura believes.

If presuppose the above four points that Katsura taught, some problems dissolved and make some hypothesis, Fukuda explained.

From these explanations, how to get the high temperature in the iron sand smelting, which has a causal relation to the production is obvious.

The reasons of the first using of the iron stone smelting then iron sand in the world history (first only iron stone was used, later they used iron sand): 1) difficulties of getting high temperature by the chemical reaction (the components which are needed for chemical reaction were not naturally included in the iron sand), 2) the yield rate of the iron production from iron sand was low, I consider. However, in Japan, iron sand smelting was popularized. The reason for this is the widely available iron sand material (wealthy, rich, abundant amount), it was possible by the Tatara (bellow). By these conditions big production was realized, with the plus and minus reason given above.

Therefore, in ancient times when they did not need mass production, they used iron stone (magnetite, hematite, and limonite). When they moved to mass production style, they switched to iron sand.

11. Bloomery Iron Method (Kaimentetsu-ho)

1) Pit-like Furnace

The iron era of Finland is 500 BC-1150 AD, consequently the iron era of Finland started 2 centuries earlier than Korean early stage of iron (300 BC- about 0 AD). Shamanistic people (Sami people-current population is about 50,000 in Northern Europe, and Lapland people) who moved from Siberia and they lived in Finland from ancient times. They smelted iron in a branch of the Aura River in the Aura Valley.

Jouko Pukkila, University of Turku, got the cooperation of a traditional knife-maker. He made a knife by smelting limonite by the ancient style pit-like furnace, in fact. See illustration 11-3. Using the charcoal for the fuel, and reduced by 1200-1300 degrees C.

Jouko Pukkila's pig iron (See illust. 11-6) was small grained such as fish roe (roe is fish eggs while still in the ovarian membrane). This is true sponge-like iron, which is like the northern method versus the southern Shoko-ho. The distribution of the kaimentetsu (bloomery iron) method and Shoko-ho (puddling method) is in the following illustration 11-4.

When I saw Jouko Pukkila's pig iron, my impressions were a little different from these 1 and 2:
1) when sponge iron stone was reduced, the stone was not smelted perfectly and many holes made by the evaporation of the oxygen from the oxygenized iron were visible, and kept shape of the sponge iron stone.(12)

stone.(12)

2) bloomery iron, which was not separated enough from the slag.

Jouko Pukkila's iron is not included so many impurities and had lovely fish roe. His iron was well smelted and did not include many impurities, making it look like lovely fish roe. High percentage carbon was included in the pig iron. I brought to Japan such

Illust. 11-1. Pit-like furnace in Korea
(Photograph presented by Chinju National Museum)

fish roe and a sample of a hammered piece of iron. I showed the swordsmiths in Japan, who told me that this is bloomery iron. He had prior experience with bloomery iron. Later he heated the iron and struck by the hammer, this bloomery iron easily went to pieces when struck.

Therefore sponge iron is from iron stone, bloomery iron is from limonite, I learned.

318

Illust 11-2. Pit-like furnace in Finland (excavted in Rovaniemi) and sectional plan (right)

(Photographs presented by Helsinki National Musuem)

According to his master thesis[9], the progress of the pit-like furnace in prehistory was the first furnace, and next was the shaft furnace which used a clay shaft in the end of

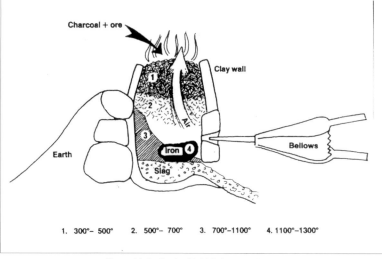

1. 300°– 500°   2. 500°– 700°   3. 700°–1100°   4. 1100°–1300°

Illust. 11-3. Jouko Pukkila's experimental furance sectional plan

the prehistory. This shaft furnace became the Cupola furnace. Iron smelting in the first stage was the direct method using charcoal and produced low carbon iron. The next shaft furnace was more effective. The material of the iron was marsh and lake ore (limonite).

According to another Finnish swordsmith, the Finnish traditional knife used limonite taken from the bottom of the lake, and smelted using the light coal. He declared we must use best quality light coal for the fuel.

The pit-like furnace, which was displayed at the Helsinki National Museum, was shown in the same situation as it was excavated. Bengara was spread all over the bottom of the furnace. See illustration 11-7 and 11-8. Hematite became the material of the iron, when the oxygen of the hematite

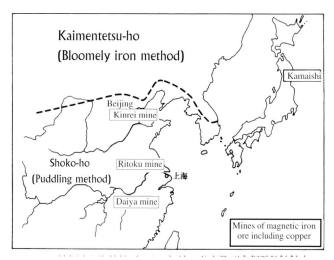

Illust 11-4. Distribution of the Shoko-ho and Kaimentetsu-ho by Mr. Hideya Okada of New Japan Iron Steel Industry Company (Shin-nihon-seitetsu)[7]

319

Illust. 11-5. The iron which was from limonite smelted by the pit-like furnace. Left to right: 3 massive stones(limonite), smelted pig iron shaped as fish roe, hammered pig iron, and knife by Jouko Pukkila.

Illust. 11-6. Smelted pig iron shaped as fish roe(biggest)

Illust. 11-7. Hematite, Bengara (colcothar)

Illust. 11-5.

Illust. 11-6.

Illust. 11-7.

was released to the air by heating Bengara was made and, therefore Bengara was spread. In Japan this research is not done, I think.

By the Jouko Pukkila's experiment, traditional Finnish knife made from limonite, includes many chemical elements, involves shaped as sponge iron, the fish roe like bloomery iron, and the high temperture made by the chemical reactions and so on. For the propulsion of the chemical reactions, not only charcoal but coal, cork, and lime, were used in ancient times.

If we think about only charcoal temperture, we cannot understand how the high temperture was attained in ancient times.

The test limonite smelting with a pit-like furnace by Mikko Flemming (Illust.11-9) and Turku University project team.

The limonite which was excavated at the bottom of the lake, was used for the traditional iron-smelting from the ancient age.

Picture 11-10: The limonite was put on the charcoal. Picture 11-11: The pit-like furnace was used the normal moisten clay, and smelted within about two hours, before the clay became dry. The furnace has a air blowing shaft near the bottom of furnace. Picture 11-12: Limonite became a iron-like-slag. From this refining is very difficult.

Illust. 11-8. Upper photo: the furnace bottom spread with bengara. Lower photo: covered furnace.

(Photopraph presented by the Helsinki National Musuem)

From upper and left to right.
Pict.11-9, -10, -11, -12

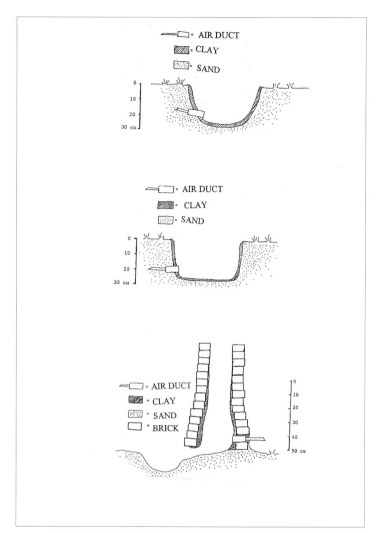

Fig. 2
Cross-section of the pit furnace used in the first experiments

Fig. 3
The best results were obtained with this kind of pit furnace which was itself a result of several experiments.

Fig. 4
A schematic cross-section of a tower furnace with a slag opening used in the experiments.

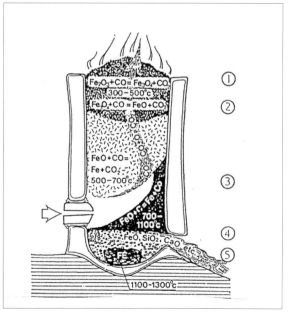

Fig. 5
A simplified presentation of the reduction process in a tower furnace.

1) Roasting zone
2) Indirect reduction
3) Oxidization
4) Direct reduction
5) Slag formation and its removal from the furnace

(Presented by Jouko Pukkila, Professor of Turku University)

321

Furnace types without slag opening

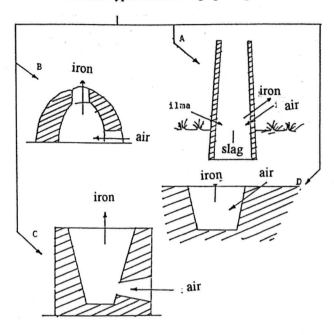

Furnace types with slag opening

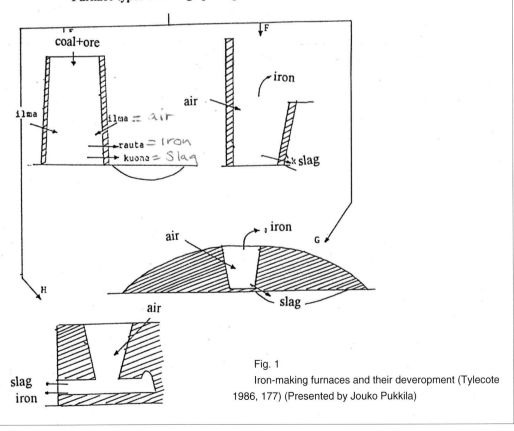

Fig. 1
Iron-making furnaces and their deveropment (Tylecote 1986, 177) (Presented by Jouko Pukkila)

2) Shaft (Blast Pipe) Furnace

In the case of the shaft furnace used for mass production, there is a medieval Sri Lankan furnace. This furnace has fourteen shafts (blast pipes) and used monsoon controlling the wind for the blast. See illustration 16. This news was announced by the Japan Times January 1996[13]. Japan Times announced the article from Nature magazine January 4, 1996.

According the Nature article, forty-one ancient blast furnaces were excavated in Samanalawewa. This excavation site was dated from 3rd century BC to medieval times. This industry was finished in the 11th century. By the archeological research, within June to September during the monsoon season, minimum 139 furnace sites had been worked in the 60 square kilometers. Founded blast furnace was first group of the iron furnace site. This site was used from the 7th century to the early 11th century. This site total production 3500 tons.

According to the field test of two replica ancient blast furnaces which were constructed by the original design used iron stone which was mined in this district which included a high percentage of carbon, and made iron. This ancient production was very good quality and traded to the other countries. From the east in Africa, Sri Lankan steel high percentage carbon was found, which included the date.

The blast furnace smelted iron stone we know because of the elements found in the slag. Every blast furnace kept high temperture continuously and produced by the controlled oxygen. Before this founding of the furnace, archeologists never thought the blast furnace was so good, because they thought natural wind was too erratic to control. Therefore they could not design a natural wind blast furnace. These blast furnace were built on the top of the hill on the west side of the summit, and distributed. This idea developed by the Sri Lanka and did not originate from India. Dr. Gill Jureff explained.

In Japan, I consider the origin of the tatara (bellow) method to be similar to these Sri Lankan shaft furnaces and made much interest. These shaft furnaces did not use mechanical bellows, but used natural wind. Natural wind is not easily controlled, but from this illustration, 16, wind, which goes beyond the high walls, suck up the wind through the blast pipe (vacuum). Therefore, air goes throughout the whole furnace. Near the blast pipe the temperture was 1500 degrees C. If the air by the hand or machinery to the lower part of the furnace, such high temperture cannot be attained. The idea such as "suck up the air like a chimney" is a ancient people wisdom. Therefore the next stage, the Cupola style, was developed.

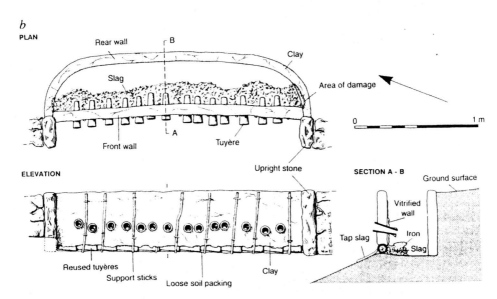

b

PLAN

Rear wall

Slag

Clay

Area of damage

Front wall

Tuyère

0   1 m

ELEVATION

Upright stone

SECTION A - B

Ground surface

Vitrified wall

Iron

Tap slag

Slag

Reused tuyères

Support sticks

Loose soil packing

Clay

NATURE · VOL 379 · 4 JANUARY 1996

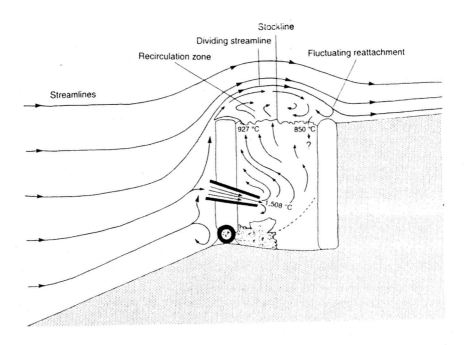

Stockline

Dividing streamline

Recirculation zone

Fluctuating reattachment

Streamlines

927 °C

850 °C

?

1.508 °C

Illust.11-13. The Iron smelting wind furnace excavated in Sri Lanka
(from the "Nature" Vol. 379, April 4, 1996)

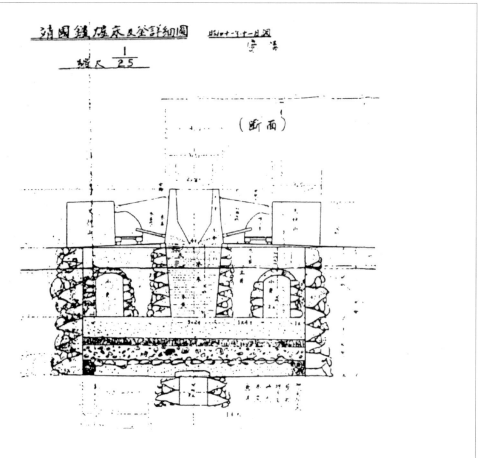

Illust. 11-14. Yasukuni Tatara Furnace for sand-iron smelting (From the "Tatara iron smelting and the scientific Japanese sword" p.43)

7) Tatara furnace

This Eidai Tatara furnace (Yasukuni tatara) is one of the most important methods in Japan, which was influenced by the Korean Peninsula, is used for smelting *tama-hagane* (*tama* means bullet, *hagane* means steel) and *Kera* (which includes steel, pig-iron and some kind of slag) in direct. The material is sand iron. After first smelting, *Kera* will be classified with some quality level.

This furnace usually avoid the water, that's why clay furnace must be wait for a month until perfect dry.

Current Tatara furnace in Shimane prefecture was made in 1977 with Yasukuni tatara furnace is in the behind of the bale in mysterious, because the current smelted tama-hagane is not so good quality.

The illustrations show some of the excavated from the ruins, but the current tatara furnace still can not rediscover the same quality like an ancient quality.

We can find some reasons why tatara furnace can reduce the high quality steel. For instance, the silicone which is included in the clay wall of tatara furnace moves to Fe, and make an eutectoid steel when this steel was treated quench hardening. The cementite, which is made from austenitic structure, in eutectoid steel is protected with the silicone and increase hardness. I consider that other phosphorus and sulphur of slag also have relation between Carbon and Fe, for making strong eutectoid steels than normal steels.

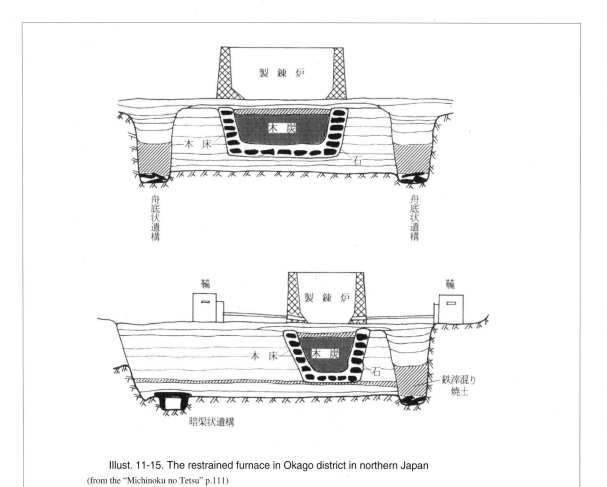

Illust. 11-15. The restrained furnace in Okago district in northern Japan
(from the "Michinoku no Tetsu" p.111)

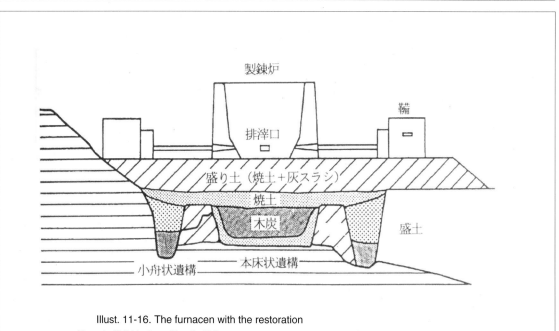

Illust. 11-16. The furnacen with the restoration
(From the "Michinoku no Tetsu" p.112)

12. Puddling method (Shoko-ho)

Shoko-ho is the contrast method of Kaimentetsu-ho (Bloomery iron method). The accurate plan was not so easy to come by. I could not find theory that explained about heating details of Shoko-ho. The next illustration was estimated and drawn by Mr. Minoru Sasaki, Phd.(15)

Mr. Masao Serizawa introduced one of the Shoko-ho styles underground circle furnace, which used a blast pipe placed within a brick cover. See illustration 12-3.(17)

I think the difference between the Shoko-ho and the Kaimentetsu-ho is the different processes of carbon removal. Eventually, Kaimentetsu-ho makes sponge iron or luppe which is not include high percentage

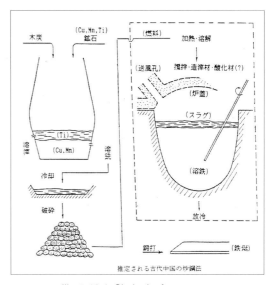

Illust. 12-1. Shoko-ho furnace
estimated by Mr. Minoru Sasaki

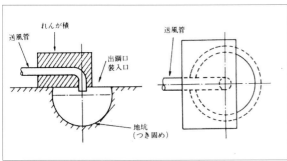

Illust. 12-2. Iron smelting furnace(16) upper)
Illust. 12-3. A kind of Shoko-ho furnace in
Shandon province, China(17) (lower)

carbon. In Shoko-ho, at the second stage, the pig iron is heated up again for removing carbon. This is a double stage method, or an indirect method. Comparing to kaimentetsu-ho, soon after smelting by Shoko-ho, pig iron is decarburized with air by puddling. By the puddling with a stick and mixing air to the pig iron, then carbon decreases. In the book entitled "Tenko-kaibutsu or Tiankonkaiwu"(16) written in China during the Ming era, 14th-17th century. The furnace drawn, the bellows are pushed by hand and he pig iron is stirred. See illust. 12-2.

The carbon removal person puddling with the wooden stick would sometimes sprinkle the shells which was burned in advance at the seashore. The reason for this was if the pig iron temperature drops and cannot be stirred easily, these sprinkled shells (calcium) would make an outbreak of gas, allowing the pig iron to be melted again, and again enabling one to add air to remove carbon. Some people understand that this calcium was used to lower the melting point, but I think this is a kind of heating, because if the shell were burned with the charcoal and the coke, it becomes carbonized calcium, and add water, making acetylene gas, or added salt to the shells.

These methods are Chinese time honored and introduced by the text book of the metallurgy school.

13. Bronze casting furnace in Xia era in China

Small furnace (size of the widest part of the pot, about 30 centimeters. From now on I will call this casting pot.) of Xia in China are displayed at the Beijing National Museum of Historical China. Peacock stone and cast bronze were shown. Natural coke , iron plate, iron stone, water bellow, charcoal, and blast pipe of Han era are shown in illustration 26. Copper-man mask and other very valuable artifacts are displayed. In November 1996, I was able to get agreement for taking photo-

Illust. 13-1. Two pictures, copper casting pot of Xia era, which was called "helmet of general."
(Photographs presented by the Beijing National Museum of Historical China)

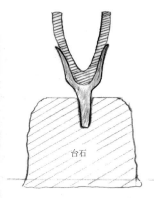

Illust. 13-2. Usage method of the copper casting pot

graphs within the museum.

I drew Illustration 13-4 by the method which was taught to me by a person who lived Fujian province, China through the help of Lujian Xing. This method is well known in China. I looked for this explanation about its use, then I could find the book entitled, "The Book of the Weapon of Historical China."(18) This book was borrowed from Fujian Teacher's University's library. The next section is a script derived from this book.(1)

Illust. 13-3 Copper-man mask (a person of Yin era)
(Photographs presented by the Beijing National Museum of Historical China, November, 1996)

1) Bronze casting pot of Yin era (Shang)

According to this book, the casting pot of the Yin era was called "helmet of the general." These methods and processes are as follows:

"Yin person cast bronze, such methods and processes were recognized by the Yin ruin archaeological section of China. This process has five stages, as follows:

1. Selection of mineral sand.

Before the putting the mineral sand into the casting pot it needs selection of clearly unnecessary stones, and other ingredients of the mineral sand must be separated. The copper sand which was found in the Yin ruins included high percentage mineral ingredient and included stones were very few. Therefore this copper sand was separated by hand. One head metallurgist tried to separate this copper sand, but he was unable to.

2. Mixture.

When the mineral stone was put in the furnace in current (current method), uses melting material for the testing of the stone. Then the copper which was dissolved like metal. Ancient people in Europe never knew about this melting material, therefore they checked by eye. Yin people were the first to know about how to use melting material, so charcoal and standardized mixture were used by the Yin person. They had a formula for the mixture, but this mixture was never known to the current people, only Shang (Yin) people for casting.

3. Tin soaking (mixing)

Copper in the furnace, this quality is very clean. But needs to be refined again. Tin, which was refined already, was soaked into the copper (bronze). Shang (Yin) people used a clay kiln. It was proved by the fact that the burned clay and about 20 kilograms of massive amount of clay was found. The pan, which was used by the Shang people, very few was excavated. They make a shape called "helmet of the general," archeologists also use this name. This shape as a helmet (Illust.13-1). This clay included crushed mica and crushed stone pebbles, and another material for earthen ware. The upper of this furnace is a pot and the lower stands on one leg. This weigh about 7 kilograms. Its capacity is about 5.4 liters. Melted copper about 12.7 kilograms can be put in. The thickest part of the furnace is 3 cm. The leg of the pot is rather pointed and its length is about 10 cm. This is so the pot will not fall over. This leg has a rather small diameter, so as it will make turning the pot easy. This is very convenient for moving the pot. These are Shang (Yin)'s method but this idea of this type of production is more ancient.

4. The forming of the mixed metal for some purpose.

Many molds were found in the Yin ruins. Therefore they had many purposes for these molds. For instance, a kind of halbert ("Ge" or "Mao" in Chinese), arrowhead, sword molds, axe head, small sword, drill head, needle, etc. were found. These have a hex sign of Totetsu (Japanese) ("Taotie" in Chinese) for decoration. Shell signs are also there. All in the mold. These molds are very intricate, with a good balanced design, very good hand work. These are not early bronze age.

5. Ornament

After the bronze was molded, it needed ornament for make beautiful goods. Shang (Yin) person decorated by hand very intricate work, making hole work, pressing work, etching work, bright work, make hard work, and keep quality work. Different people have each job like burnishing. These were very high level techniques. ("The Book of the Weapon of Historical China"(18), page 61-62)

By Chinese chronology, Xia era is 21-16th century BC, if these casting pots were transfered from more ancient times, this time would be same as the Japanese Jomon early middle stage or more older. This era in Japan, Kassaka-style Jomon pot and Otamadai-style pot were distributed throughout the Kanto and Chubu area.

2) The Components of Bronze Weapons

The casting furnace that melted the copper used mainly bornite (peacock stone) for material. It would make copper first and then other melted materials (metals) were mixed.

Current chemical data of bronze includes Copper (Cu) 88-98% and Tin (Sn) 2-12%. Bronze is useful for molding as well as art, and coins. In Xia era, I consider it was primarily used for hunting weapons. Yellow copper includes copper 60-70%, Zn 20-40%. This character is yellow and very strong and resistant to rust.

If I consider why this mixed copper was made in ancient time, the most reasonable answer is to keep from rusting. Eventually in case of hunting at sea, bronze or yellow bronze weapons would not rust as much as iron. Hunting material is very important for life. When using the mixing techniques of bronze for iron, as iron stone or sand is easier to find than bronze material, they could make iron. (The ancient people thought bronze was best because iron would rust too easily.) Therefore I think ancient time they used bronze or yellow bronze for hunting.

If they used iron, we need for find some reasons like that iron making is easier than bronze. For instance, once hunting race's population increased they would need many weapons and they would have to switch from hunting small fish and animals to bigger ones, like whales, killer whales, or dolphins for their food. Another reason for the switch is fighting one another. If they need iron material before the bronze era, they could smelting iron. If in Japan iron was smelted, there are reasons for using iron material.

The broken copper-man masks, which were excavated in the Shu dynasty (Chengdu city in Sichuan province) are very big and heavy, requiring many people to lift. Big mulberry tree, which was used for harvesting silkworms, which has a many branches made from bronze, about 3 meters high. The people who made the copper-man masks moved to the east where the sun rises. They had bronze plate, where bird on the background of the sun was painted. The sun was brought by the bird, this type of thinking, Chinese archeologists think. Shu dynasty was very famous for the fighting of the three kingdoms. But, we do not understand where the strong fighters came from. From the early era of this country started the fishing with cormorants (cormorant is a diving bird with webbed toes), this cormorant was not leashed, but worked only by the fisherman's order. The Shu dynasty character means eye and silkworm, but the eye means copper-man's eye, and the mask was also mask's eye stuck out. This report was given by NHK television in 1995, and in 1998 there will be an exhibition in Japan named "Mysterious golden mask exhibition." If they moved from China to the east, it was considered that they visited the island of Japan.

"The Book of the Weapon of Historical China" explained about a helmet, which was made in the Yin era, as follows:

"The inside of the helmet, red copper remained. Outside colorful and bright luster, Zinc and nickel plating, maybe. Shang (Yin) era is bronze alloy era."

Before this book was published, 10 or so years ago, Mr. Wan, president of Beiping Geological Survey Institute, and Mr. Guanyu Liang, staff of the institute, analyzed a bronze arrowhead as follows:

Shang era Bronze Arrowhead   **Bronze Arrowhead excavated from Yin ruin**

330

Copper	28.09%	39.0%
Iron	2.16%	1.14%
Tin	5.60%	10.71%
Silver	very few	-
Lead	very few	-
Oxygenated Silicon	3.66%	
Silicon Iodide	-	7.39%
Water	-	(?)
Carbon Iodide	-	(?)

In this table, copper has a rather low percentage, but iron, tin, lead, and silver are alloy. Tin people were accustomed to use these metals.

In the spring of 1931, England Royal Industry Academy mining professor Sir H. C. Harold Carpenter analyzed more precisely then took the following table:

Kind	Red Copper	Tin
sword	85.00%	15.00%
arrowhead	83.00%	17.00%
?weapon?	80.00%	20.00%
ceremonial artifact	(?)	10.20%

From this analysis, the tin component is rather high, but the alloys were very precisely measured and this percentage is almost same as current percentages.

3) The Principle of Shoko-ho

I sent the illustrations (Illust. 13-4), which I consider how to use the carbonic acid gas, to the Wuhan Iron Steel Institute through Wuhan Institute of Physical Education. I received a reply explaining that in ancient China carbonic acid gas was continually used throughout the smelting process. Therefore, clearly my illustration is not in error. When smelting bornite, if using this gas, molding is without problems.

The illustrations show pouring the water into the pot and putting it into the burned carbide, which is lime stone, with charcoal. This generates acetylene gas. From the top, they would put burning coals to light the acetylene gas. Boiling water makes oxygen through evaporation. The oxygen is separated from the hydrogen, therefore the acetylene gas would burn with a strong flame.

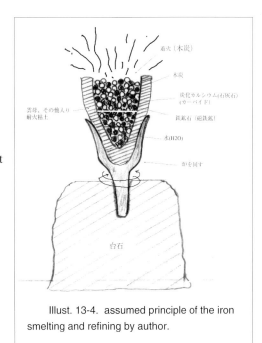

Illust. 13-4. assumed principle of the iron smelting and refining by author.

Water not over 100 degrees C protects the pot from cracking. After the water evaporates, add more little by little and then the carbide is also added.

In the illustrations show when the iron is smelted. After smelting the iron stone continuously rotate the pot aerating the pig iron, removing the carbon, and strengthening the acetylene gas flame.

The principle of the Bessemer converter was founded in Germany by Sir Henry Bessemer. Until his discovery in the 19th century, nobody this discovery before.

If using carbonic acid gas in the smelting pot like the illustration, and oxygen, I think 1600 degrees can be achieved. Therefore, the Chinese furnace was developed using this principle.

When attention was given to iron instead of bronze, this principle was changed to shoko-ho.

14. Casting Furnace (Standing) in Shang and West Zhou eras

1) Standing Bronze Casting Furnace

According to the book, "Chinese Bronze Goods"[34], during the Shang and West Zhou era (16 century BC to 771 BC), in China, very large casting were done unexpectedly. This book explains about Chinese bronze goods and castings in the Lushang mining ruins of Dayelian city in Hubei province.)

The next explanation is translated by Lujian Xing and myself.

In 1973, a red copper axe and many wooden supports were discovered. This was a strip mining site from ancient times. In 1974, an old cave was discovered, from the south to the north 2 kilometers in length, east west 1 kilometer. Near the cave there was a buried furnace. The slag, which was 1 meter underground, totaled 400,000 tons. The slag analysis of the copper percentage was 0.7% and the iron was 50%. The original mineral stone analysis, copper was 12-20%, while iron was about 30%. The bornite in the copper was 20-50%. Original mined red copper stone was conjectured total 400,000 tons, and copper was reduced after refining was amount 40,000 tons (the "Dictionary of Chinese Findings and Discoveries", Wuhan Publications 1995, explained that the total production of various minerals of this ruin was 800,000 tons).

By the measurement of the ruin's era by the Carbon 14 dating, this cave was used in the late Shang era through the Chunqiu era and Warring State era until near a little before the Early Han era (until about 210 BC). When this cave was used, the method of mineral vein discovery was already developed. According to the observation, natural copper was bornite with this color, and the finding by the luster of the mineral stone. They used a Feng Shui compass to locate the mineral veins. Wooden compass was used for searching the vein, but not only used for direction but also searched angle for finding the cardinal points. The element components could be measured by use of this compass. The quality of the different veins could be separated into three levels: top, middle, and poor class. They then could decide which vein to mine. With this method they could be sure that they would mine only the rich veins. They would mine up to 50 meters underground.

The structure of the Lushang mining ruins were shaft cave, drift style, and diagonal, all supported by wooden props. When the cave was first mined, the shafts were only wide enough for crawling, but later it became wide enough for upright walking. The vertical shaft cave, used a wooden square floor-ceiling boards with wooded supports. If they couldn't find a good deposit, they would then change to the drift cave or diagonal cave. In the diagonal cave, standardized angles were used. This angle had a relation to the angle of the vein and water drainage. In a cave used in Chunqiu era, a bronze axe, wooden hammer, large wooden boat-shaped container, and a bamboo bowel, wooded level, etc. were excavated. At the cave of the Warring State era or Late Shang era, iron hammer, iron axe, iron hoe, other iron tools, and other bamboo instruments, and wooden hooks, wooden logs used for transportation were excavated. These materials were used for mining, measuring standard in the mining process. In this cave, there is flat bamboo, which was rather small and burned, which they probably used these for torches. This cave was believed to be for clean air. Entrances were made on different levels to create a flow of air.

From this mountain, many slag at the Northeast slope, 8 furnaces for copper, a part of the furnace wall, the copper ingot (pig copper), mineral stone, charcoal and heat resistant materials were excavated. The shape of the furnace is standing (vertical), which was constructed with 3 sections: basement, furnace cylinder, and furnace shaft. The basement of the furnace in Chunqiu era was underground with air vents. The upper part of the cylinder section also contained grooves (perhaps used to fasten the shaft to the cylinder section). The shaft stands on top of the cylinder section. From these remaining parts of the furnace, the archeologists could not reconstruct a working model. Around the Daye Lake, about ten pieces of copper ingot formed circles. These types of ingots are called "rice-cake". One of these ingots weighs about 1.5 kilograms. According to the analysis, copper was 91.86% in these ingots. However, the mold for the bronze casting could not be found. Perhaps they were cast at Lushan mountain in Daye city and brought to Daye lake. The site of the Lushan mining cave is a convenient location for distribution. This lake is near the mountain. Lake Daye was through to the Yangzi river and copper transported to other locations in China. The discovery and excavation of this ruin is very important for the archeological history of ancient China's production, for correct understanding. Chinese Shang, West Zhou era bronze casting and mining metallurgy development were proved through this discovery. The district of Daye were within the ancient Chu dynasty's borderline and this mountain included the Chu dynasty and very high level casting in East Zhou era are proved.

From this book, it allowed me to understand that the standing shaft furnace was used for copper casting and produced bronze, and throw out iron (not needed) as slag. Therefore, when bronze was cast, it was possible that iron could be reduced from iron stone and could achieve the high temperature for the iron reduction in the furnace, but they never recognized the value of the use of iron. Therefore, iron was thrown away. I especially noticed in the slag that the iron (30-50%) percentage was higher than the copper percentage. (The iron here in the slag was thrown away, not used, after the reduction process, therefore the high percentage). It is regrettable that the standing furnace illustration was not shown in this book.

Table of various metal's melting points (degrees C)

W....3400	Os....3045	Ir....3400	Cr....1860	Pt....1770	Fe....1450	Co....1490
Ni....1450	Mn...1240	Cu..1083	Au...1064	Ag.....962	Ca.....839	AL.....660
Mg....649	Zn......420	Pb.....328	Sn......232	Na.......98	Ka.......64	Hg.......-39

2) Standing furnace to the blast furnace (development into large blast furnace)

During the Chunqiu and Warring States eras of China, clay made standing furnace, which used heat resistant materials, produced bronze. Only the Daye copper furnaces produced 400,000 tons of slag in mass production were done.

A large amount of iron was consumed in Warring States era. The furnace became big, and the bellows used hydraulic power, that could achieve high temperature for smelting and get a high yield rate. This method was exported to Europe.

The furnace drawn in the book, Tenko-Kaibutsu (16), was rather bigger and the bellow was pushed by two people, but in the Chin and Han era there were the biggest furnaces used, recorded in the book.

The next pages show the shaft furnace in Han era.

The standing furnace of Japan which was used for casting bronze go back to the early middle Yayoi era. The standing furnace excavated in Akita prefecture dated back to the 9th century.

Illust. 14-2. Small standing furnace in Akita prefecture. Kanninzawa ruins,furnace #1, 9th century (23).

Illust. 14-1.
From the upper to lower: Coke, iron stone, iron plate, curved blast pipe, hydrolic powered bellows, furnace wall (all in Early Han era)
(Photographs presented by Beijing National Musuem of Historical China)

3) Heap Roasting for Desulfurization

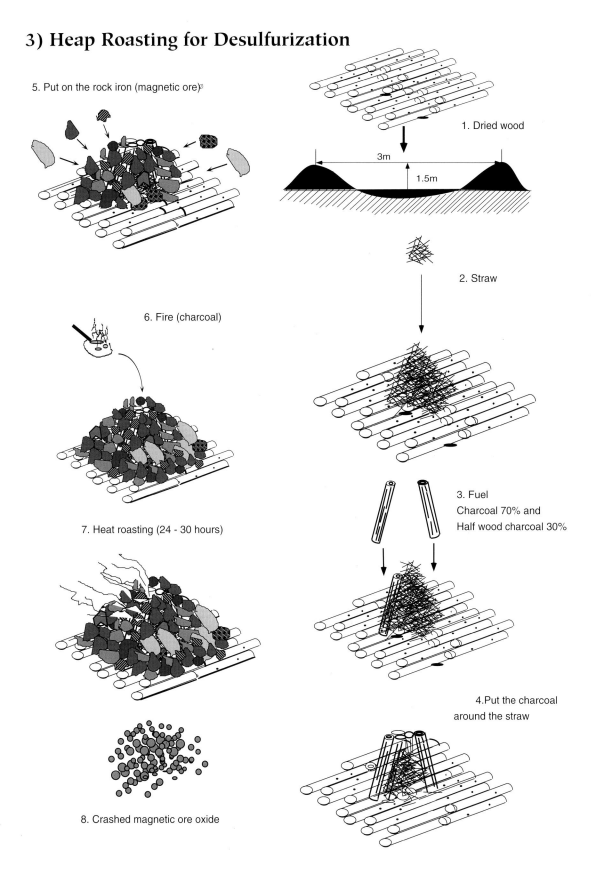

5. Put on the rock iron (magnetic ore)

1. Dried wood

3m

1.5m

2. Straw

6. Fire (charcoal)

3. Fuel
Charcoal 70% and
Half wood charcoal 30%

7. Heat roasting (24 - 30 hours)

4.Put the charcoal
around the straw

8. Crashed magnetic ore oxide

335

4) Smelting method with Chinese Casting furnace

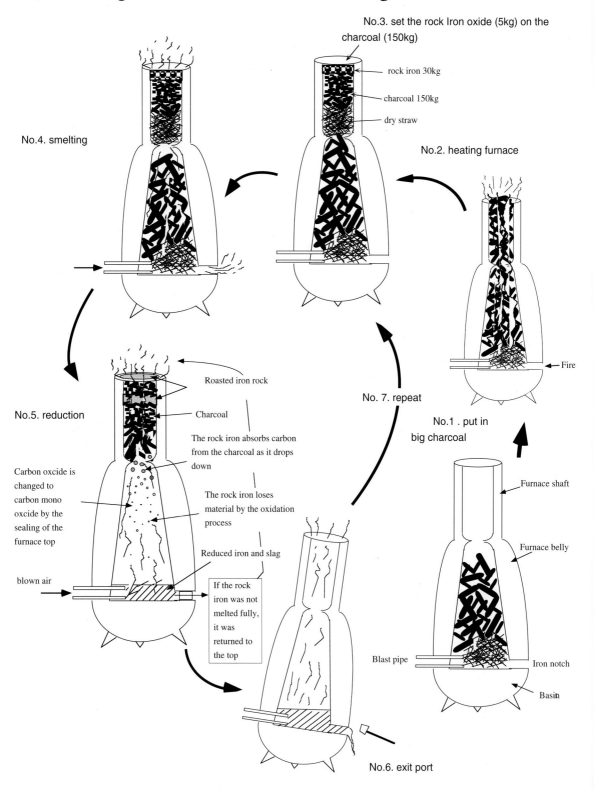

No.3. set the rock Iron oxide (5kg) on the charcoal (150kg)

rock iron 30kg

charcoal 150kg

dry straw

No.4. smelting

No.2. heating furnace

Fire

No.5. reduction

Roasted iron rock

Charcoal

The rock iron absorbs carbon from the charcoal as it drops down

Carbon oxcide is changed to carbon mono oxcide by the sealing of the furnace top

The rock iron loses material by the oxidation process

Reduced iron and slag

blown air

If the rock iron was not melted fully, it was returned to the top

No. 7. repeat

No.1 . put in big charcoal

Furnace shaft

Furnace belly

Blast pipe

Iron notch

Basin

No.6. exit port

336

4) The detail of the Chinese casting furnace in Han era (B.C.6C-A.D.3C)

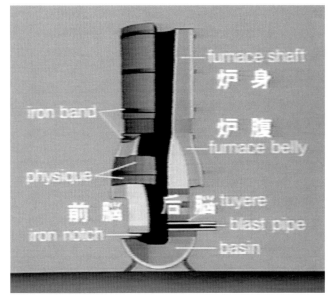

Illust. 14-3. Furnace profile

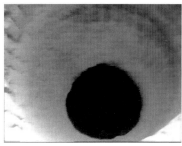

Illust. 14-4. The lower part of the furnace shaft

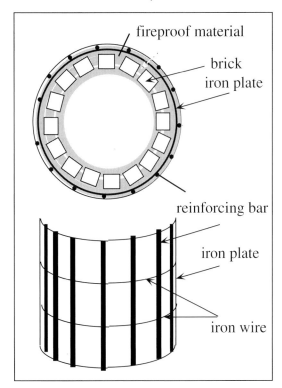

Ullust. 14-7. Inside of the furnace shaft

Illust. 14-5. The bottom of the furnace

Illust. 14-6. The furnace belly

15. Jomon Pot

1) Style and Quality of the Jomon Pot

Bronze produced in China during the Xia era was during the middle of the Japanese Jomon era. Archaeologically, this is considered when there was no Japanese techniques on the island of Japan. When it

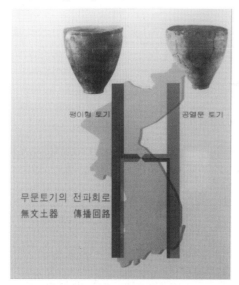

Illust. 15-1. Korean "no-crest" earthen vessels, which were influenced by Chinese pots and Japanese Jomon pot.
(Photographs presented by Chinju National Museum, Korea, 1997)

became Yayoi era (3rd century BC to 3rd century AD), iron was brought from the mainland. After that, iron production began. Therefore, Japanese iron era was delayed for about 8 centuries compared to China, 14 centuries from the Hittite empire. This is the common opinion of archaeological historians.

I consider that the cultural exchange was continues between Japan and the mainland, especially during the mid Jomon era and the Yayoi era show these influences strongly. I especially notice this relationship in Korean earthen vessels (pots). In Korean history, after the Old Stone Age (30,000 - 10,000 BC), there is a gap, but in 5000 BC started the New Stone Age, then the "comb crest" earthen vessel culture era (5000 - 1000 BC). This was then continued to the Early Iron Age (300 BC - 0). "Comb crest" earthen vessel changed to earthen vessels without any designs. My question is why the "comb crest" design was lost in the Early Iron Age.

Koreans "no-crest" earthen vessels were modeled after the influence of the Chinese vessel and the Japanese Jomon vessels. This was how the Korean Chinju National Museum explained. See illustration 15-1.

The Early Iron Age in Korea, the earthen vessel became "no-crest" by the Japanese and Chinese influence. Then, in the Three Kingdoms era, box-shaped furnace was made.

I think the Jomon pot which was used for smelting is not decorated with handles or faces, but very simple "no-crest" earthen vessels.

2) Excavated Smelting Pot

The pot excavated in Hokkaido

Next picture shows an earthen vessel excavated in Rausu Town on Shiretoko Peninsula in northern Hokkaido (Illust. 15-2).

This pot seems to be of the Okhotsk-style, 5th century, which used blast furnace, achieving up to 1100 degrees C. Northern people's (northern culture explained in the first section) Evanki race (one of the Tungus

Illust. 15-3. Iron smelting (?) by the Evanki of the Tungus race, photograph by Mr. Kazuyoshi Otsuka.

(The original photograph explained that the Evanki blacksmith was forging, but it seems to me that use of a bellow testifies to him smelting and not forging.)

Illust 15-2.
Upper: Okhotsk style pot, used for iron smelting, excavated at the Sashirui North coast in Rausu.
Left: The original shape of Okhotsk style pot.

races) used the pot for smelting. They used acetylene gas in the shoko-ho.

Whether to use the pot on top of the ground or partially underground is decided on the volume of the pot. Shoko-ho means "stir steel method" from the Chinese. Therefore, the image is the stirring of the smelted iron, thereby refining the material. The image is of using chopsticks to stir. Why change the method from rotating the pot to stirring the smelted iron, in the second refining stage? I think when the iron is smelted, if using water inside the pot, the pot sometimes may break from the heat, therefore they changed to the pot being buried, plus

Illust. 15-4. Forging by the Sakhalin Ainu (Original illustration is by "Kitaezo Zusetsu", Illustration Book of Northern Hokkaido)

339

placing clay inside the pot. They could not rotate the pot, since it was buried, so they changed to the stirring method. If the pot would crack under the ground, the material would not easily spread out, still being contained in the hole. In the buried pot, acetylene gas would be generated inside, then refining is done with the stirring of the stick. This method uses the same principle as the bronze casting in Shang era.

If using only charcoal as fuel and aerating from above (illust. 15-3) one cannot achieve high temperature making it impossible to smelt the iron stone or iron sand. The impossible is made possible with the addition of the acetylene gas being generated. Shoko-ho, using the buried pot or casting material such as a buried bowl, is used for small smelting production. This method was popularized throughout China. Northern horse-riding people cast metal from the Shang era, as shown at the exhibition held Horse Museum in Yokohama city. This exhibition was named "Horse-riding People on the Steppes: Bronze of Northern China" (March 25-May 5, 1997). This type of smelting continues to today. This casting bowl is called "Sand Bowl" today.

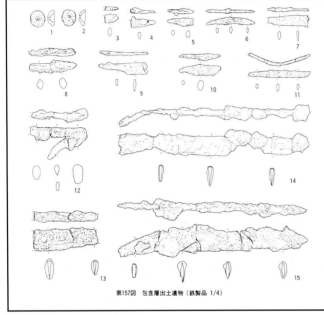

第157図 包含層出土遺物（鉄製品 1/4）

Illust. 15-5. Excavated iron knives from the Menashidomari ruin.(36)

It is repeated that during the Satsumon period in Hokkaido, Sakhalin Ainu used the pot for smelting without the aid of a blast pipe (Page 339(23)). I believe limited iron production in Hokkaido used the shoko-ho pot.

This chart was made by Mr. Hideo Akanuma. These iron materials mainly used iron stone and used sand iron to decrease the carbon percentage in the pig iron, Mr. Akanuma explained

遺物名	出土地	T.Fe	Cu	Mn	P	Ti	Si	非金属介在物組成	原材料	脱炭材
蕨手刀	モヨロ貝塚	62.89	0.030	0.002	0.108	0.018	0.441	F＋T	含りん	砂　鉄
鉄　斧	〃	70.69	0.429	0.001	0.410	0.008	0.165	—	含　銅	—
鉄　鉾	〃	68.78	0.002	0.006	0.019	0.004	0.142	W＋F＋D	鉱　石	鉱石粉
直　刀	〃	61.03	0.026	0.022	0.385	0.153	1.85	T＋D	含りん	砂　鉄
刀　子	美々8	66.96	0.012	0.006	0.045	0.050	0.446	T	—	砂　鉄
不明鉄器	釧路5	59.76	0.095	0.004	0.190	0.025	1.037	—	含　銅	—
不明鉄器	〃	59.30	0.004	0.012	0.072	0.035	2.239	—	—	—
不明鉄器	〃	57.86	0.007	0.005	0.167	0.057	0.594	T	含りん	砂　鉄

Table 3.

Table 3. Analysis of the iron goods in Okhotsk Satsumon period(26)

3) The Era of the Jomon Pot including Mica

Otamadai style pot (Omigawa town, Katori district in Chiba Prefecture, Japan) includes mica within the clay. Some of the excavated Jomon pots seemed to be used for smelting. I hope to research at a later time (this research should Otamadai style pots). Some pots, which includes mica, were excavated in Okinawa island (Kaneku style pot), and Itoman city. This era goes back to the Yayoi era, therefore these pots were transferred from the Kyushu district. If the survey was mainly executed about the Otamadai style pot, which related to the Kassaka (used in Kanagawa prefecture as well as others) style pot.

4) Concerning Mica

Mica is a silicate mineral. It's growth is similar to the pearl's growth. Most mica is included in granite and is easy to peel off. The different kinds include white, black, gold, iron, and silk. The characteristics includes a high resistance to electricity and heat. It is used in light bulbs. In Japan or China, it is used as a pigment in painting. Archealogically, in Japan mica has been said to be used in pots as a strengthen. I do not think mica's purpose was not as a strengthen, since mica is easy to break. It is weak against pressure.

5) Heat Resisting Jomon Pot

Some of the Jomon pots were used for smelting purposes. These pots would include mica, but I also think it includes other minerals such as chromite and tungsten in the clay. This adds to its heat resisting power. I hope to find data on the Jomon pot's components. I have been so far unsuccessful. Perhaps the data exists somewhere, but I have been unable to locate any.

Biratori town, Saru district, Hokkaido, Japan, the Ainu people's sacred ground is famous for its chromite mines. Usually chromite vein are very deep underground. If the chromite appears on the surface of the ground, or within a river, there are very few. I find it very interesting why the Ainu people selected a chromite mine for their sacred ground.

On the Asian continent, the "silk road" and the "steppe route", the bridges between the Eastern and Western cultural exchange, the whole route is a vein for the chromite and tungsten. Starting from Turkey, through Istanbul, the Black Sea, the Karakoram Mountains, finishing in Beijing. This is the "steppe route", and is a vein of tungsten. The "silk road," starting from Turkey through Dunhuan and ending in Japan, has a chromite vein throughout its route. The "sea road," through the Persian Bay to Beijing, is also a chromite vein. Therefore, the "silk road" is a mineral vein.

The Ainu people's sacred ground is an extension line of the "silk road". It seems that the Ainu people had a relation to the trading between the North and the South of the "silk road," trading various minerals. Ainu people have traded through the Sakhalin with the Tungus people. They also traded with Central China people (the people between the Yangzi river and the Yellow river.) This was reported at the symposium held at Sapporo Gakuen University (25). This trading time goes back to China's Yin era (16th century - 11th century BC).

6) The making of carbide and acetylene gas

Carbide is not made only by limestone, it is also possible to use seashells. There are some methods for combining carbon. The next method that follows is one of these carbide making methods:

Making Carbide

a) Burning charcoal (coke or coal can also be used), put the limestone into the fire. The burned limestone combines with the carbon, and becomes carbide.

b) When making charcoal inside the kiln, at the same time place the limestone inside the kiln. The limestone will then become carbide.

Illust 15-6.

Illust. 15-7.

Totetsu (protect gods)(illust. 15-6) is a ancient Chinese animal in the mythology, this was transfered to Buddhism and became the Japanese Oni (devil). This character has both eyes are Yin and Yang. One eye sticks out while the other eyes sticks in. Yin means negative and Yang means positive. Jomon pot (illust. 15-7) one eye seems to be the same as the Totetsu. The other eye is closed.

Kanto (left) and Chubu (right) area

c) Make a special kiln, burn only the limestone using charcoal as fuel. If one is producing much iron, a special kiln is needed for producing carbide. Therefore, one furnace would be for iron, while another kiln would be for the limestone, making carbide.

Making Acetylene Gas

a) Pour about 2 liters of water into a pot, about 30 centimeter circumference. Place the carbide (limestone) into the water. The carbide must be of such amount as to have more volume of carbide than water. The limestone sticks far out of the water. Place burning charcoal on top of the limestone. This will generate gas, which then can make temperatures as high as 1600-2000 degrees C.

b) Carbide needs oxygen to become acetylene gas, therefore, the water and pot is heated beforehand, then the evaporated water produces oxygen and hydrogen.

7) The Use of the Jomon Pot for Smelting and Refining

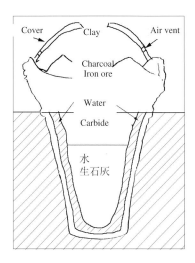

Cover　Clay　Air vent

Charcoal
Iron ore

Water

Carbide

水
生石灰

Smelting Iron Stone

Stick the wet clay to the inside of the Jomon pot, and place into the ground as in the illustration 34. Pour water into the pot, place the carbide within until sticking out over the water level. Then put the iron stone with the burning charcoal on top of the carbide. After the smelting of the iron stone is finished, the pot is either rotated or the material is stirred with a wooden stick, thereby refining the pig iron. This then becomes steel.

Illust. 15-8. The estimated illustration of the Jomon pot being used for smelting, by author.

8) The Use of the Jomon pot and crucible smelting (Similar to Indian Wootz)

This method used for the second refining stage, break pig iron into small pieces and moisten them. Wrap them into small clay vessels (place into small pot and cover with clay), and place the many small clay wrapped pig iron into furnace (Jomon pot) and heat up. This method is useful for not changing the percentages of the different elements within the material (Amalgam method). The heating fire does not touch the material. This method is not only used for iron, but lower melting point materials. This wrapping around the material would keep the lower melting point materials from evaporating, losing the metals within. Please see the section on the Indian Wootz steel again for further information.

9) Concerning the Use of Iron Sand

The following is my idea of how to use iron sand for smelting.

a) The iron sand and the charcoal powder is mixed with water in a bowl. After drying, the material becomes similar to iron stone. Then smelting can be done in a fashion of iron stone smelting.

b) After smelting the iron stone, it becomes pig iron. At the second refining stage add the iron sand to decrease the carbon. This is the carbon removal treatment.

c) Iron sand formed into a ball, as made in a), mix with a mixed ratio to the iron stone, then smelt.

16. The Iron Material in Medieval Japan

1) Production method of iron material

Mr. Hideo Akanuma (Iwate Prefecture Museum) announced the academic report (26) on the type of Warabite sword excavated from Northern-northeast Japan and Hokkaido area. Over 60% of the Warabite swords excavated in Japan come from this area, versus the remaining 40% coming from the other parts of Japan. He researched the material of this type of Warabite sword, and was also able to separate the swords into 3 different categories with their respective locations.

Mr. Akanuma analyzed ten Warabite swords excavated from the Kanto, Tohoku, and Hokkaido areas. He arranged as follows:

The Iron Material of the Late Kofun era (3rd to 7th century AD)

p Warabite sword (Mr. Masakuni Ishii's sword shape category #2 and #3) excavated in Kanto area.........Made from iron stone.

p Warabite sword (Mr. Masakuni Ishii's sword shape category #1) excavated in Tohoku area.........Made from primarily iron stone, but including some iron sand.

p Warabite sword (Mr. Masakuni Ishii's sword shape category #1) excavated in Hokkaido area.........Made from primarily iron stone, but including some iron sand.

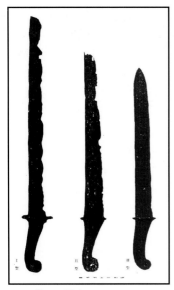

Illust. 16-1.
Mr. Masakuni Ishii's
warabite sword shape category
(from left to right, category #1, #2
, #3)

Warabite Sword Characteristics of the Late Kofun era

Both a pot as well as a sword were excavated together, by determining the date of the pot, the sword date was also determined.

The iron material made in the early middle 7th century excavated from Kanto, Tohoku, and Hokkaido use the iron stone as the original material. The iron sand was added to the iron material from the middle of 7th to the end of 7th century in the Kanto area. In the Northern Tohoku district, this practice was started from the end 7th to the early 8th century. In the middle in the 7th to the end of the 7th century, a large iron working center was made in the Kanto and Tohoku district. Archaeologists were correct with their theory of the different variations of iron stone. The variation of the material of the iron stone in the iron goods fit as archaeologist's opinion.

The Quality of the Iron Goods Excavated in Northern Tohoku district and Hokkaido area with the Heian era to Medieval Times.

Titanium is usually included in iron sand, but not in iron stone. This is the determining factor when deciding whether the material used in a sword came from iron sand or iron stone. At this time, the excavated iron goods included the usual percentage of titanium. Therefore, iron sand was used for adjusting the carbon in the process of making steel. It was

344

added to the pig iron, which was smelted from magnetite which included phosphorous. According to this fact, Eastern Japan's end of ancient time smelting method was not of the direct variety. The indirect method was used.

This clarifies that in the Heian era a group of high level technique iron-mongers, lived in Northern Tohoku district, working for iron production. Within the middle of Heian and the late Heian era, the ingot which included phosphorous and magnetite, was widely distributed from the Kanto area to the Tohoku area.

Analysis of Iron Goods from the Okhotsk and the Satsumon culture in Hokkaido

The iron goods in this time period, some included the primary material being copper-included magnetite (iron stone). Yet other goods other metals were also detected including high percentage phosphorous, titanium, and steel.

The Quality of the Medieval Iron Bowl and Iron Goods

Especially in Hokkaido, the iron bowl was popularized, being used for cooking, instead of a clay pot. After the analysis of this type of iron bowl, it was clarified that this iron bowl included a high percentage of phosphorous and the original iron stone was phosphorous including magnetite. This type of iron bowl differs from the bowls found in the Nibutani, Ainu sacred ground, and O'hamanaka ruins. 70% of the iron goods were made with the phosphorous including magnetite. According these points, in the Heian era, iron goods was transferred by the trade to the Northern Tohoku district and Hokkaido. Mr. Hideo Akanuma's analysis of iron slag and iron goods, which were made with phosphorous including magnetite, points to this.

Iron technical groups who made high phosphorous titanium included steel in the Heian era, whether the steel was wholly made in Japan, or only the second stage was done in Japan (the first being done on the Asian continent and imported to Japan) is not totally known.

In the Medieval age, these iron bowls

Illust. 16-2. Earthern bowl excavated in the Sankhalin Island
(Hakodate City Museum)

Illust. 16-3. Estimated iron smelting using iron bowl in Medeival age by author

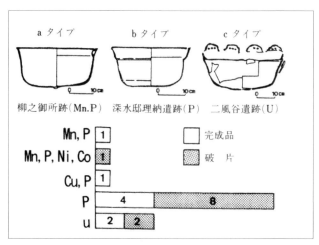

Illust. 36. Formation of the excavated iron bowl in Medieval age (by Mr. Hideo Akanuma)[27].

had ear-shaped hooks on the inside. When this style bowl started or where this shape came from is not understood. The Northern horse-riding people made bronze bowls which had similar ear-shaped hooks on the upper edge of the bowl in the Shang era. Therefore, the origin of the Japanese iron bowl has a relation to the Northern continent. I think these iron bowls were used for iron smelting in the shoko-ho style.

17. Mizuhodo (Water Furnace)

Japanese blast furnace which was started in the 19th century was introduced to Japan from Korea, and was established in Kamaishi city. At this time, concerning this introduction, the government introduced through the work of the Nanbu feudal clan and the Sendai feudal clan. After smelting with the blast furnace, the pig iron was refined through a water furnace (Mizuhodo), resulting in Nobetetsu (high quality knife iron (wrought iron, Carbon, about 0.1-0.2 %.)(Knife Sword). The yield rate of this pig iron refining furnace was approximately 75-90%. This was a very high percentage reduction. This iron was sold to the Fukushima district and used for farmers equipment in Northern Tohoku (Aomori prefecture). The name of the store was "Mizuhodo-ya," and is still used to this day. This principle of Mizuhodo is similar to the Chinese shoko-ho.

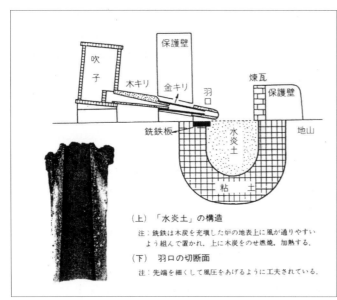

Illust. 17-1. Mizuhodo.

Mr. Kokichi Okada explained about the Mizuhodo as follows (28):

Mizuhodo is similar in structure to the pot with a diameter was about 30 cm and the depth was about the same. First time, insert charcoal made from chestnut into the water furnace, then add about 1.8 liters water. The charcoal become wet. Prepare water in another pot. On the Mizuhodo, burn the charcoal, the heating of the pig iron removes the carbon. At the same time, before the process, the ingot which already had carbon removed, was already at the bottom of the furnace. Three process continuously worked in this furnace. (Heating, smelting, refining: a pre-stage, the first stage, and the second stage.) See illustration 17-1. Pig iron must be heated in advance. Three workers in one day can produce about 64 kilograms, which yielded a rate of approximately 80%.

After smelting, there are two kinds of iron, zuku (pig iron with a high percentage of carbon) and kera (steel with a lower percentage of carbon).

After taking only the steel used for sword, lower carbon steel, there remains high carbon pig iron. There are then two processes (*Sageba* (remove carbon) and *Honba*). There are 6 workers. The yield rate is 60%. One day production is about 187.5 kilograms.

346

If we compare both Mizuhodo and tatara-ho, mizohodo method has one extra process, but the mizohodo production is smaller than tatara. The tatara needs extra carbon removal (Sageba). If we compare the number of workers, the yield rate, and quality of production, and process of both the tatara and Mizuhodo, Mizuhodo is better. From a technical and economical point of view, Mizuhodo is better.

Mr. Kuniichi Tawara, appraiser, said that this mizuhodo influenced modern smelting techniques, and improved the method.

After reading this script, I telephoned Mr. Kokichi Okada. He emphasized the yield rate of the mizuhodo is 85-90% and its economical superiority. Concerning fuel, he denied any relation to China. He said this method is Aomori district's own techniques.

However, from this illustration, I don't think that the wet charcoal would burn when the burning coals are place upon them. I don't think high temperature can be attained with this method. He mistook not putting limestone in. If limestone (carbide) is placed in the mizuhodo, generating acetylene gas, perhaps this furnace would work. The reason for the high percentage yield rate would be from the high temperature of the acetylene gas. Therefore, it seems that the Chinese casting furnace in the Xia era of shoko-ho is also high yield rate. Mr. Kokichi Okada explained one process of preheating the pig iron, is not pig iron, but limestone.

The mizuhodo in Aomori district is applied method of the iron bowl in medieval age and iron smelting Jomon pot. Later, if the clay pot was excavated from the iron production ruins, there needs to be research done on whether limestone or seashells (calcium) were there. If, in the case of the sulfur and niter was chemical reaction in the furnace, temperature become near 1700 degrees C, and niter would become glass. So it is possible to find glass characteristic in the slag at the excavation sites.

18. Conclusion

If use the Japanese Jomon pot, iron reduction or smelting were possible from iron stone (limonite, magnetite) and iron sand. The Jomon pot used was either buried under the surface or top of the ground and is something I cannot clearly understand.

The Chinese casting furnace in Xia era, using an earthen vessel, used watering to protect the vessel from breaking from the high temperature. The evaporated water produced oxygen, spurring on the flame increasing the temperature. This is a very reasonable method. This method developed into shoko-ho, using the clay wrapped iron balls. This method was transferred through the Korean peninsula and all of Siberia and North Europe. Colcothar (hematite) was used as a source of oxygen instead of from water, I presume. The box-style furnace is a kind of this colcothar-using style furnace.

From Yayoi era in Japan, shoko-ho and kaimentetsu-ho were developed both in unison. After the introduction of tatara-ho from other countries, iron sand was smelted in the large clay-made furnaces. (Iron sand was used because of the large production and iron sand is plentiful in Japan) Therefore, ancient method (shoko-ho) was slowly diminished until being almost totally lost. The small furnace of tatara-ho grew to the Eidai tatara (meaning permanent furnace), which then developed into the current blast furnace, going back to iron stone with this style.

The development of the furnace in China and Japan are in order as follows:

(China):
Small structure smelting:

1) Standing the pot in the stone method (bronze, gold, silver, iron: in Xia era)

2) Buried pot in the ground, with clay wraps inside pot method (shoko-ho) starting from Shang era.

3) Buried or placed on the ground iron bowl with clay wrappings inside (still using today, by minority races)

Large structure furnace:

1) Standing (vertical) furnace with iron material inside (24) small clay pots (copper, iron. From Late Shang through West Zhou through Chunqiu to Warring States era)

2) Large tank style furnace (inside of the pig iron furnace is heat resistant clay wrappings) (copper, iron: from Qin era to Han era)

3) Blast furnace high copula style (steel: from Han era to current time)

(Japan):
Small structure furnace:

1) Half-buried sharp bottom earthen vessel or On-the Ground flat bottom earthen vessel furnace (copper, iron...From Kanto to Northern Tohoku and Hokkaido) mid-Jomon era to Zoku-Jomon era in Hokkaido

2) Box-style furnace (iron) early Yayoi era

3) Standing vertical furnace (bronze, iron) Yayoi era or Kofun era (if the pig iron is wrapped in clay and then place into standing furnace and refine, this is similar to Rutsubo-ho)

4) Clay-wrapping iron bowl (iron, Tohoku, Hokkaido, medieval age) The medieval iron bowl was transferred from the Asian continent through Sakhalin and Hokkaido to Tohoku, it seems.

5) Clay-made furnace called tatara-ho (iron... From Izumo district and moving North in Japan) about 5th century

Large structure furnace:

1) Eidai Tatara-ho...Modern age (indirect method)

2) Blast furnace high copula (introduced from Korea, used Tatara-ho) (1st stage smelting and 2nd stage refining were separated. This is the indirect method) 19th century.

I arranged the order of the different furnaces and their times after my long research. In the case of Japan, the foreign separation is easy to understand, as the following:

Jomon era (earthen vessel), Yayoi era (box-style furnace), Kofun era (shaft furnace, and standing furnace), medieval age (iron bowl, iron sand tatara-ho), after 19th century (blast furnace, and converter)

My thinking when I saw the excavated box-style furnace, I could not decide whether it was only for kaimentetsu-ho or make circular pit in central furnace and use this furnace as Shoko. Eventually I remembered the direct method box-style furnace in the Finnish early iron age. I hope there will be more research done about this.

If I conjecture about the ideal sword steel, it includes high percentage of manganese from the iron stone, low percentage of titanium or high percentage vanadium. These are mixed special steel. If it does not include other materials and aim for only pure iron to make steel, is not so good you should expect. Also I think for removing the impurities, keeping a continuous high temperature (1400-1500 degrees C) is needed.

348

Through the use of additional chemical elements, these reactions will remove the impurities. For instance, decreasing sulfur niter should be used. For removing calcium, limestone should be added. These ancient rational methods will be solved in the future through academic research.

The hard-bodied sword (Dao or one-sided blade), which is used for Baguazang (a kind of internal-body boxing style) uses hard steel for material, and other flexible double-sided blade (Jian or Ken) which uses the soft steel (low percentage of carbon) needs temper (placing carbon only on the outside), Kejian Zhang told me. When I visited the Chinese sword factories in Longquan city, Zhejiang Province, China, they would not agree to my seeing how they placed the temper to the blade. I could not confirm what Mr. Kejian Zhang said. According to Kejian Zhang's explanation, temper is that one time put into the water, then quickly pulled out, and then placed into oil. This oil included melted lead and a little gasoline. The melting point of lead is 328 degrees C. This is hot, cold, then hot again. This is the method for adding temper.

Footnotes & Bibliography

(1) Ludwig Beck, "History of Iron", translator Morito Nakazawa, (publisher Yonago Tatara Shobo, 1968-1986), 19 volumes.

(2) Morito Nakazawa, "The Position of Japanese Smelting Techniques in the World History"

(3) Richard F. Burton, "The Book of the Sword" (Dover Publications, 1987, N.Y.)

(4) Kameki Kinoshita, "Mineral Stone Pictorial", (Hoikusha Publications, 1995)

(5) "An Instance of Titanium Composite: Possible use for the blade", (Kobe Steel Industrial Company, Jan. 1987)

(6) Toshio Kato, "New Materials and the Knife", Knife Magazine, Feb. 1997

(7) "The Journal of Swords," magazine, Issue 318, July, 1983

(8) Iron Smelting History Research Association of Tokyo Industrial University, book "Ancient Japanese Iron and Society," page 223-238, Author Kei Katsura, article "The principle of sand iron smelting" (publisher, Heibonsha, 1982)

(9) Same book as above, but page 167

(10) Hideya Okada of Shin Nippon Steel Industrial Company, article "The Distribution of the Shoko-ho and Kaimentetsu-ho", magazine "The Journal of Swords," , Issue 318, July, 1983

(11) Jouko Pukkila "IRON SLAG AND IRON WORK IN THE AURA RIVER VALLEY DURING THE IRON AGE" University of Turku), 1996

(12) Masao Serizawa, article "What is Ancient Chinese Shoko-ho?", magazine "Metal" Vol. 54, No. 5, page 46-47, 1985

(13) Japan Times Jan., 1996.

(14) "Nature" magazine, Jan 4. 1996

(15) Minoru Sasaki, "Ancient Iron from the View of Metallurgy", Editor: Tatara Research Association. Book: "Iron Production of Ancient Japan," page 47, Rokko Publishing Company, 1991

(16) Song Yingxing,   Book: "Tiangong Kaiwu" Translator Kiyoshi Yabuuchi (Heibonsha Publication, 1969)

(17) Masao Serizawa, article "What is Ancient Chinese Shoko-ho?", magazine "Metal" Vol. 54, No. 5, page 48, 1985

(18) Wei, Zhou "The Book of Weapons of Historical China", (Xinhua Publishing Company, 1957, Beijing)

(19) Tetsutaka Sugawara, article "Ainu Sword and the Jomon Pot", magazine "Mogusato-Kenkyukiyo", Vol. 6, Mogusa Sword Research Association, 1997

(20) The Officially Approved Textbook of the Education Ministry, "Chemistry" Jikkyo Shuppan Publications, 1987

(21) Bessemer, H., An Autobiography (Office of Engineering, 1905)

(22) The Officially Approved Textbook of the Education Ministry, "Chemistry" Jikkyo Shuppan Publications, 1987, page 165

(23) Photogravure (front pages photo), Editor: Tatara Research Association. Book: "Iron Production of Ancient Japan," Rokko Shuppan Publication, 1991

(24) "The Dictionary Mac Kojien", software 1994 version 4

(25) Edited by Sapporo Gakuin University Department of Civilization, book: "Hokkaido and Minority People" article "Open Lecture on Hokkaido Culture", August 20, 1993

(26) The script for the Northern Iron Culture Symposium, title "Considering the Northern Culture through Iron", page 61, Nov. 3, 1990

(27) Hideo Akanuma, "The Components of the Iron Material Production Excavated from Castle Ruins", magazine "Seasonal Archeology" Vol. 57, page 55, Yuzankaku Publishing Company, Nov. 1996

(28) Kokichi Okada, article "The Blast Furnace Smelting of Kamaishi Iron Mines and Wrought Iron Production", edited by Shin-Nihon-Seitetsu Company, Public Information Section by Shin-Nihon-Seitetsu Company, title: Second Volume of the History of Iron Culture, page 96,

(29) Isamu Taguchi, Yasuhiro Ozaki, book: "The Iron of Michinoku" Agune Technical Center, 1994

(30) Uno Harva, "Shamanism: The World-View of the Altaic Races", Sanseido, 1989

(31) Editor: Masao Ota, "The Book of Taoism" Gakushu Kenkyusha, 1993

(32) Editor: Masao Ota, "The Book of Shugendo" Gakushu Kenkyusha, 1993

(33) Shiro Akane, "The King of Ancient Eastern Japan: A Study of the Kamitsu-Kenushi Family" Publisher: Asaosha, Gunma Prefecture 1988

(34) Chief Editor: Ma Yongyuan "The Chinese Bronzes", Shanghai Old Book Publishing Company, Aug. 1994

(35) Kokichi Okada, article: "Iron Smelting around the Mount Kitagami", book: "The Iron of Michinoku", Agune Technical Center, 1994, page 36

(36) The Menashidomari Ruin, the report of the Archeological Excavation accompanied 238 National Road Improvement Construction organized by the Esashi town Educational Committee, 1994

Magnetic susceptibility measurements and mineral composition of red ochre samples from Finland

Site	Description	Susceptibility (10-3 SI)	Mineral composition*
1. Harjavalta	grave	9.4-12.9	Hem+Qrz+Smc+Fldsp
2. Vantaa	soil cont. by red ochre	1.8	Smc+Qrz+Fldsp
3. Ilomantsi	natural (?) red ochre	20.8	Qrz+Fldsp+Smc+(Hem)
4. Kaustinen	natural (?)red ochre	1.0-4.5	Plg+Qrz+Hem
5. Laukaagrave		14.8-15.6	Hem+Plg+Smc+Mag+Pyrr
6. Luakaasoil	soil cont.by red ochre	1.1	n.d.

Legend

* Mineral composition is based on x-ray diffraction analysis, excluding sample no.5 which was also investigated with thermomagnetic analysis.
Minerals: Hem = hematite, Mag = magnetite, Pyrr = pyrrhotite, Qrz = quartz, Plg = plagioclase, Fldsp = feldspar, Smc = smectite
n.d. = not determined
(Presented by Helsinki National Museum, Finland)